THE LITTLE MUSIC LOVER'S FIRST PIANO LESSON

The Perfect Piano Book for Beginners

MARINA J. LLYOD

TABLE OF CONTENTS

CHAPTER 1 – MUSIC THEORY

LESSON 1 - Music and the Staff	1
LESSON 2 - Clef (Treble & Bass)	1
LESSON 3 - Musical Notes	2
LESSON 4 - Note Values	5
LESSON 5 - Rests	7
LESSON 6 - Bar (or Measure)	7
LESSON 7 - Time Signature	8
LESSON 8 - Finger Numbering (Fingering)	9
LESSON 9 - Grand Staff	9
LESSON 10 - Ledger Line	10
LESSON 11 - Notes on Piano	11

CHAPTER 2 – PIECES & STUDIES

STUDY A.1	12
STUDY A.2	13
STUDY A.3	14
STUDY A.4	15
STUDY A.5	16
LITTLE BO PEEP	17
MARY HAD A LITTLE LAMB	18
GIRLS AND BOYS COME OUT TO PLAY	19
LIGHTLY ROW	20
A-TISKET, A-TASKET	21
BINGO	22
TWINKLE, TWINKLE, LITTLE STAR	23
HICKORY DICKORY DOCK	24
TEN LITTLE INDIANS	25
YANKEE DOODLE	26
THE MUFFIN MAN	27
NEW WORLD	28
LA DONNA È MOBILE	29
O MIO BABBINO CARO	31
OLD MACDONALD HAD A FARM	33
HOT CROSS BUNS	35
PEASE PORRIDGE	36
THE STORM	37
THE BLUE DANUBE	39
STUDY B.1	41
STUDY B.2	42
STUDY B.3	43
STUDY B.4	44
STUDY B.5	45
ALOHA OE	46
FÜR ELISE	47
CAN - CAN	48
SHE'LL BE COMING ROUND THE MOUNTAIN	50
CLAIR DE LUNE	51
POMP AND CIRCUMSTANCE	53

TABLE OF CONTENTS

DON GIOVANNI	55
HEAD, SHOULDERS, KNEES AND TOES	57
IF YOU'RE HAPPY AND YOU KNOW IT	58
LULLABY	59
CAMPTOWN RACES	60
ODE TO JOY	61
JINGLE BELLS	62
ROCK-A-BYE BABY	63
AMERICA THE BEAUTIFUL	64
GREENSLEEVES	65
AURA LEE	67
AMAZING GRACE	68
THE WHEELS ON THE BUS	69
SWAN LAKE	70
STUDY C.1	72
STUDY C.2	73
STUDY C.3	74
STUDY C.4	75
STUDY C.5	76
BIG BEN	77
JACK AND JILL	78
I'M A LITTLE TEAPOT	79
SAKURA	80
ROW, ROW, ROW YOUR BOAT	81
LOOBY LOO	82
HUMPTY DUMPTY	83
STUDY D.1	84
STUDY D.2	85
STUDY D.3	86
STUDY D.4	87
STUDY D.5	88
CANON IN D MAJOR	89
POP GOES THE WEASEL	90
GO TELL AUNT NANCY	91
WHEN THE SAINTS GO MARCHING IN	92
SPRING	93
JOY TO THE WORLD	95
SKIP TO MY LOU	97
ARE YOU SLEEPING?	98
HAPPY BIRTHDAY	99
THIS OLD MAN	100
LONDON BRIDGE	101
SHAVE AND A HAIRCUT	102
THREE CHINESE WITH A DOUBLE BASS	103
SILENT NIGHT	104

CHAPTER 1

MUSIC THEORY

Lesson 1: Music and the Staff

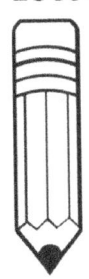

In school, you use the letters to write words. When first learning to write you use ruled paper.
The same thing happens with music. Music is written on five lines called a Staff.
The Italian composer Guido d'Arezzo created this system to write down the melodies and music.

A staff is a set of 5 horizontal lines which looks like this:

```
5 ―――――――――――――――――――――
4 ―――――――――――――――――――――
3 ―――――――――――――――――――――
2 ―――――――――――――――――――――
1 ―――――――――――――――――――――
```

Tip! Always count the lines of the staff from the bottom up.

Lesson 2: Clef (Treble & Bass)

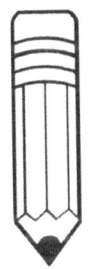

A Clef decides which notes the staff's lines and spaces represent.

Treble Clef   **Bass Clef**

The clef determines where each note sits on the staff.
They are placed at the beginning of the music line which is called...
Yep! The Staff.

We will see how these work in a few more pages.

Lesson 3: Musical Notes

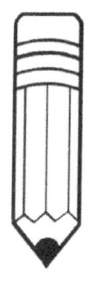

The musical alphabet, called Notes, is placed on the staff's five lines or in the space between the lines.
Just as you use letters of the alphabet to write, musical notes are combined to create music.

There are seven musical notes, each with its own name.

They are: A   B   C   D   E   F   G

Did you know that the keys on your piano are called these seven names?

Let's see on the piano:

Each group of notes repeated is called an Octave.

Look at the pattern of black keys on your piano; each octave has a group of two and a group of three.

This pattern helps us locate the notes on the piano.

For example:
Every white key on the left side of the black keys in groups of two, is: C

Can you locate all the C notes on your piano?

But what are the black keys!?

The black keys are different notes too, but they don't have their own name. We call them using the white key's name instead. Let me show you how.

Imagine we want to name a note between the note C and D, like the picture below:

We can call this note two ways:

C Sharp

or

D flat

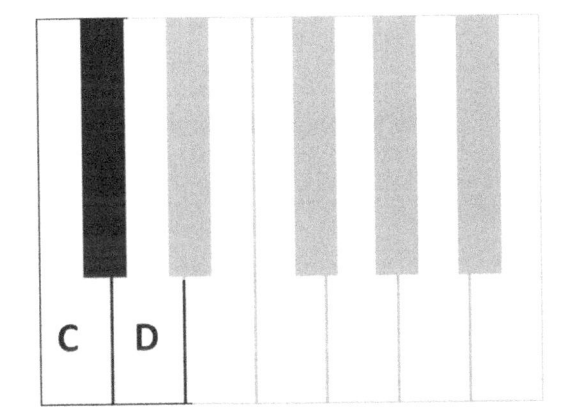

To write the black note's name on the Staff, we use the music alphabet. There are musical symbols dedicated for the word Sharp and Flat:

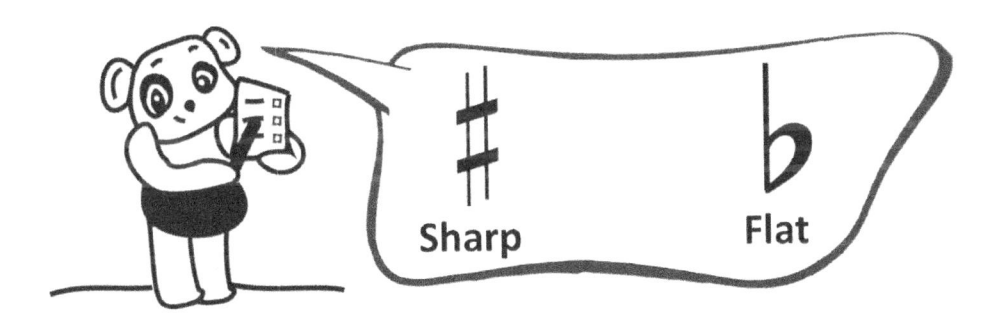

♯ Sharp   ♭ Flat

Now we know all the keys' names on the piano. Let's see the notes' names together again, just for an Octave. As you know, in all other octaves, the note's name just repeats.

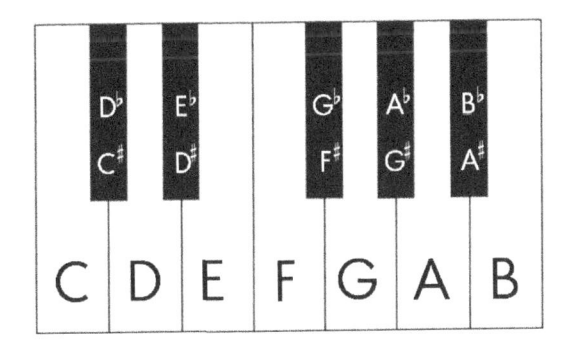

Now let's go back on the **Staff** and see how the five lines and the clef work together to show us the notes.

Here is how that works:

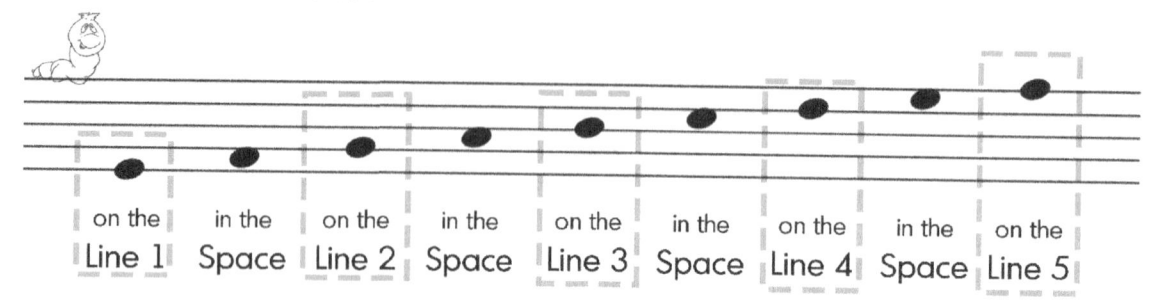

on the Line 1 | in the Space | on the Line 2 | in the Space | on the Line 3 | in the Space | on the Line 4 | in the Space | on the Line 5

Still, we don't know the names of the notes on the staff, until the Clef is placed.

- With a Treble clef, **line 1** will be dedicated to E. In the space between **line 1** and **line 2**, the next note apears which is F. And so on.

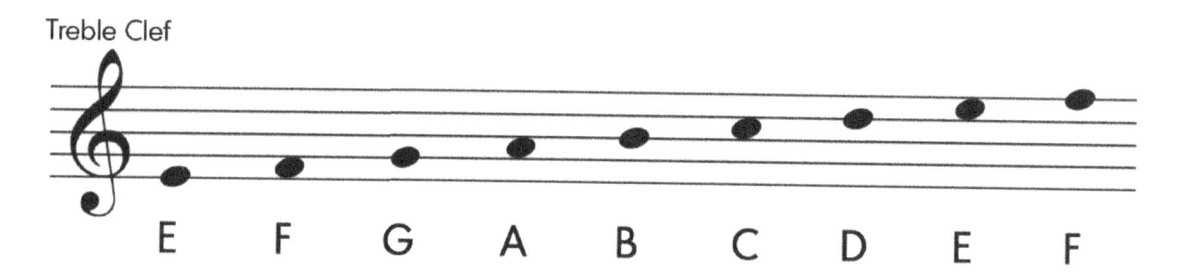

Treble Clef

E F G A B C D E F

- And with the Bass clef, **line 1** will be dedicated to G. So in the space between **line 1** and **line 2** the next note is **A**. And so on.

Bass Clef

G A B C D E F G A

Simple tips to remembering notes in the spaces

A C E G   F A C E

4

Lesson 4: Note Values

A note value is the time that a note sounds.

The value symbols are:

- *The first and the biggest one is:*

  𝕆   Name: **Whole Note**
  Value: **4 beats**

- *Next one is half of the previous one in value:*

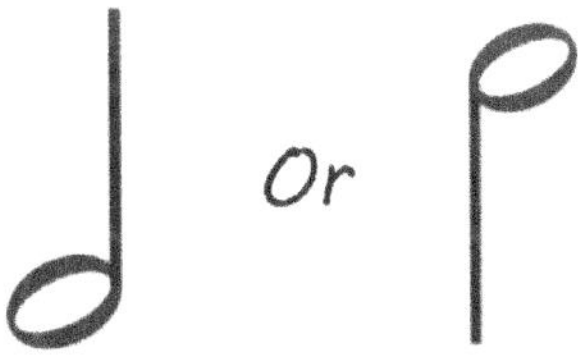

  𝅗𝅥 Or 𝅗𝅥   Name: **Half Note**
  Value: **2 beats**

  So: 𝕆 = 𝅗𝅥 + 𝅗𝅥

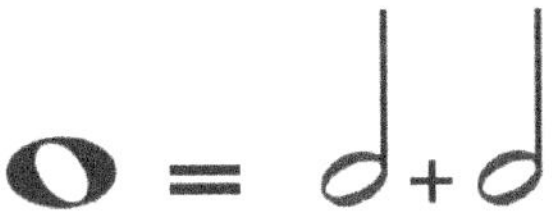

- *Next value symbol is:*

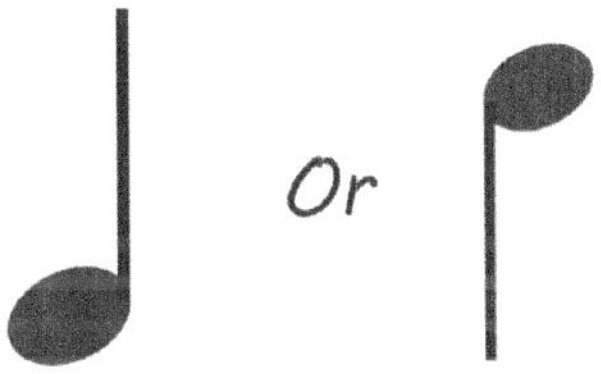

  ♩ Or ♩   Name: **Quarter Note**
  Value: **1 beat**

  So: 𝅗𝅥 = ♩ + ♩

- *The last one is the smallest:*

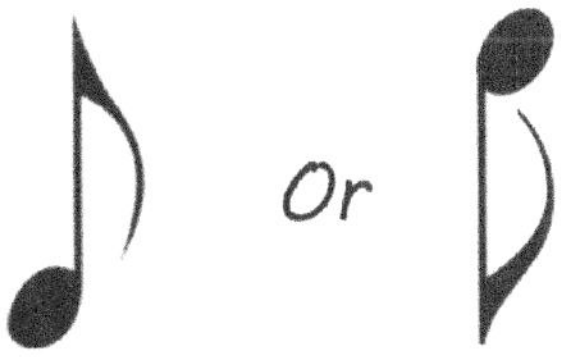

  ♪ Or ♪   Name: **Eight Note**
  Value: **½ beat**

  So: ♩ = ♪ + ♪ ≫ ♫

As you see, we have a value symbol for 4 beats, 2 beats, 1 beat and a half beat. But what if we want to show 3 beats? For example, 1 ½ beats?

To have them, we use two other symbols, which are:
- **A dot:** A simple dot that comes beside the note. The dot increases the value of the note by half of its own value.

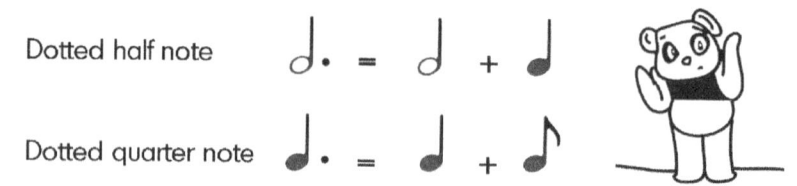

Dotted half note 𝅗𝅥. = 𝅗𝅥 + ♩

Dotted quarter note ♩. = ♩ + ♪

So, for example, if you would like to have a note for a value of 3 beats, you can easily write a half note with a dot:

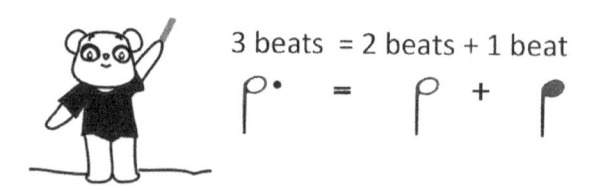

3 beats = 2 beats + 1 beat

- **A Tie:** A tie is a curved line that connects two of the same notes. A tie means to hold the note for the combined value of the two notes as if they were one.

Now let's see how we can make a note with the value of 3 beats, this time with the Tie symbol:

3 beats =   2 beats + 1 beat

Let's do something fun! Let's make a weird value like 7 ½ !

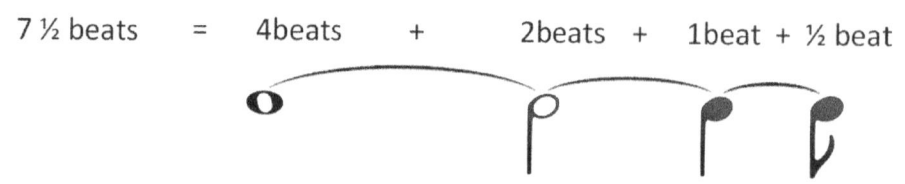

7 ½ beats   =   4 beats   +   2 beats   +   1 beat + ½ beat

As you can see, you can add as many ties as you want.

Lesson 5: Rests

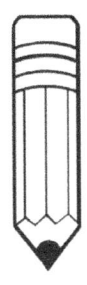

Music notes tell us when to play. A rest in music tells us when **not to play**. Rests represent silence in music.

Every note value has its own rest symbol too. Here is the table of every note value and its rest on the staff:

	Note	Rest
Whole note (4 beats)	𝅝	𝄻
Half note (2 beats)	𝅗𝅥	𝄼
Quarter note (1 beats)	𝅘𝅥	𝄽
Eighth note (½ beats)	𝅘𝅥𝅮	𝄾
Dotted half note (3 beats)	𝅗𝅥.	𝄼.
Dotted quarter note (1 ½ beats)	𝅘𝅥.	𝄽.

Lesson 6: Bar (or Measure)

A bar is one small segment of music that holds several beats. Multiple beats make up a bar and multiple bars make up a song. The number of beats in a bar depends on the time signature of the song. We'll look at time signatures in the next lesson, but for now let's see how we do the segmentation.

Bars are divided by vertical bar lines, indicating the beginning and end of the bar. Like the staff below:

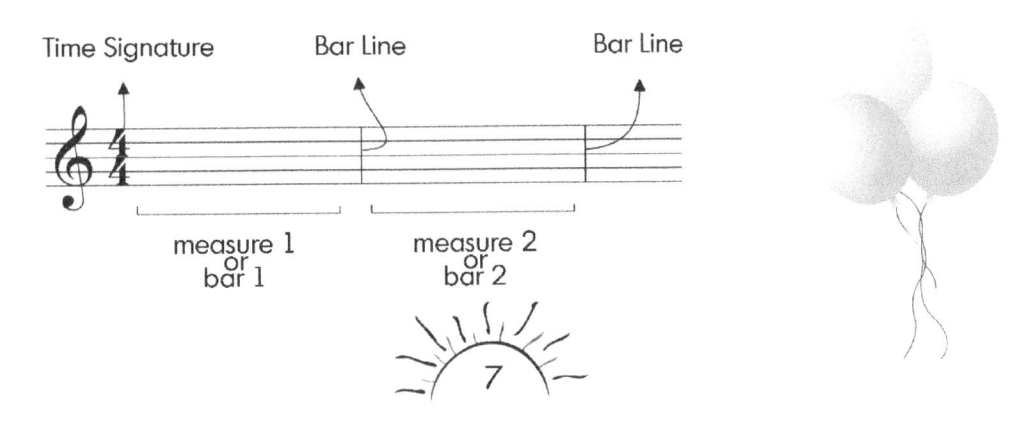

Time Signature | Bar Line | Bar Line

measure 1 or bar 1 | measure 2 or bar 2

Bar lines can be in different shapes like these:

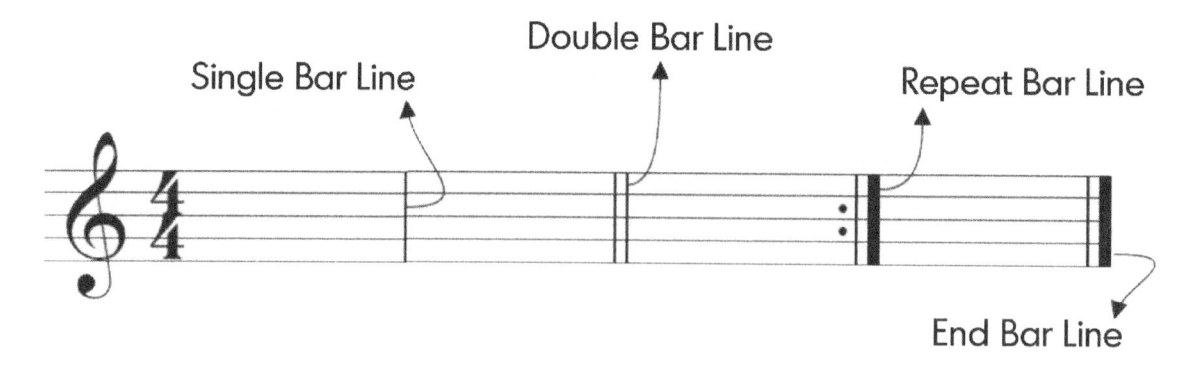

Single Bar Line   Double Bar Line   Repeat Bar Line

End Bar Line

Lesson 6: Time Signature

Time signatures specify how many beats are in each measure. Time signatures are shown as two numbers on top of each other. The upper number shows how many beats in each measure, while the lower number shows the value of each beat. For example, if the lower number is 4, then each beat is a quarter note.

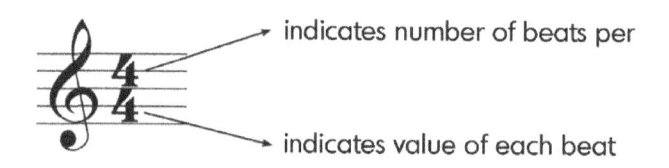

→ indicates number of beats per

→ indicates value of each beat

Here are some examples:

This means every measure can have 4 beats in total, not more or less.

quarter note = 1 beat   half note = 2 beat   2+1+1 = 4 beats
1+1+1+1 = 4 beats   2+2 = 4 beats

And here we have a 3 on the time signature that means every measure has 3 beats.

1+1+1 = 3 beats   dotted half note   2+1 = 3 beats
3 beats

And here we have 2 beats in each measure.

1+1 = 2 beats   half note 2 beats   half note = 1/2 beat
0.5+0.5+1 = 2 beats

Lesson 8: How to Play

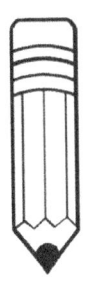

- *Finger numbers:*
  Every finger has a specific number:

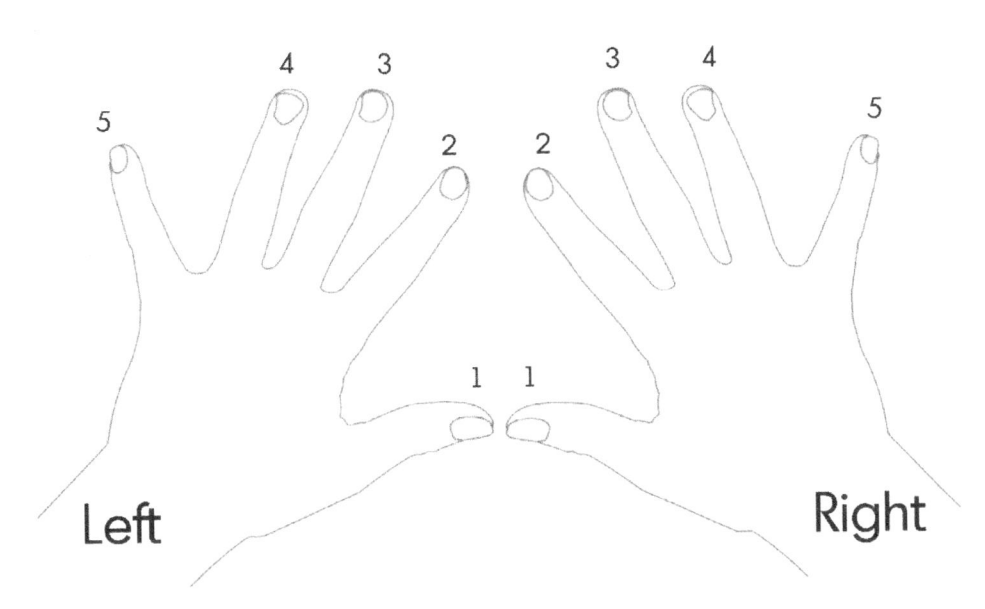

Left   **Right**

Check out the next chapter where the songs begin: above each note, there is a number that shows which finger we use to play that note.

Lesson 9: Grand Staff

Some instruments are played with two hands, like a piano. For these instruments, we need a Grand staff. The Grand staff includes two staves on top of each other. The upper line is for the right hand, and the lower line for the left. The last few exercises in this book are on the Grand staff, and we will use both hands to play the songs.

Upper line is for the right hand →

piano

Lower line is for the left hand →

Lesson 10: Ledger Line

Let's look again at the notes on the staff and count them together:

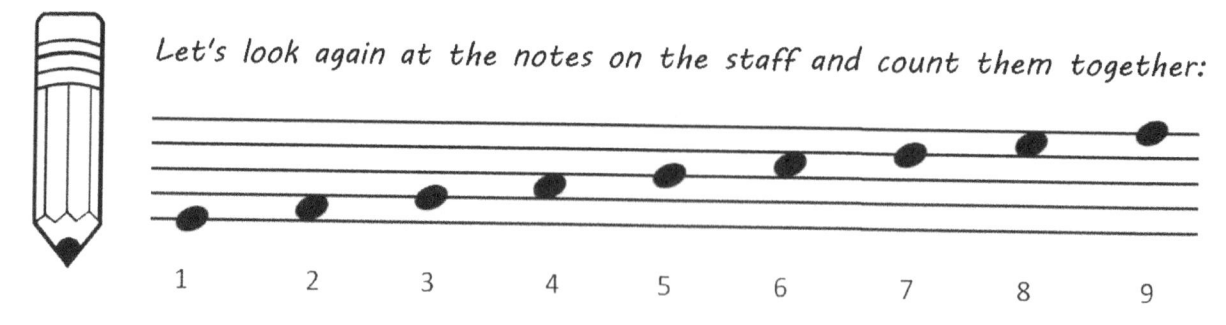

1 2 3 4 5 6 7 8 9

So we have 9 notes on each staff. On the Grand staff, the number of notes is 9+9, which is 18 notes.
But in music, we have many more notes that need to have their own place. As you can see on your piano, there are over 18 notes; each key on the piano is a note.
This is why we use leger lines to make more seats for other notes when needed.
Leger lines are small lines added above or below the staff to create additional space for other notes.
These lines are a continuation of the staff. They are used to represent notes that go beyond the lower and upper limits. See the example:

Ledger lines

Other notes with leger lines

the notes that have already a place for themselves on the staff

Other notes with leger lines

A B C D E F G A B C

F G A B C D E

When you see these lines, imagine this figure. Keep counting the notes the same way you did on the staff. Each space or line is a different note.

Lesson 11 : Notes on Piano

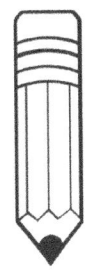

To find the place of each note on the piano, first, we must find the **Middle C** notes on the staff with each clef (Treble and Bass):

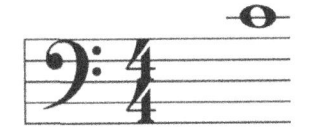

Middle C on Treble clef staff   Middle C on Bass clef staff

- Now sit at the center of the piano.
- As you remember from lesson 3, The key of C sits directly at the left of the first black key in each group of two black keys.
- Then identify the C closest to the middle of the keyboard.

This is the middle C on piano

You have found the middle C on the piano and on the staff. Now we can find any other notes, counting from this note on the piano.

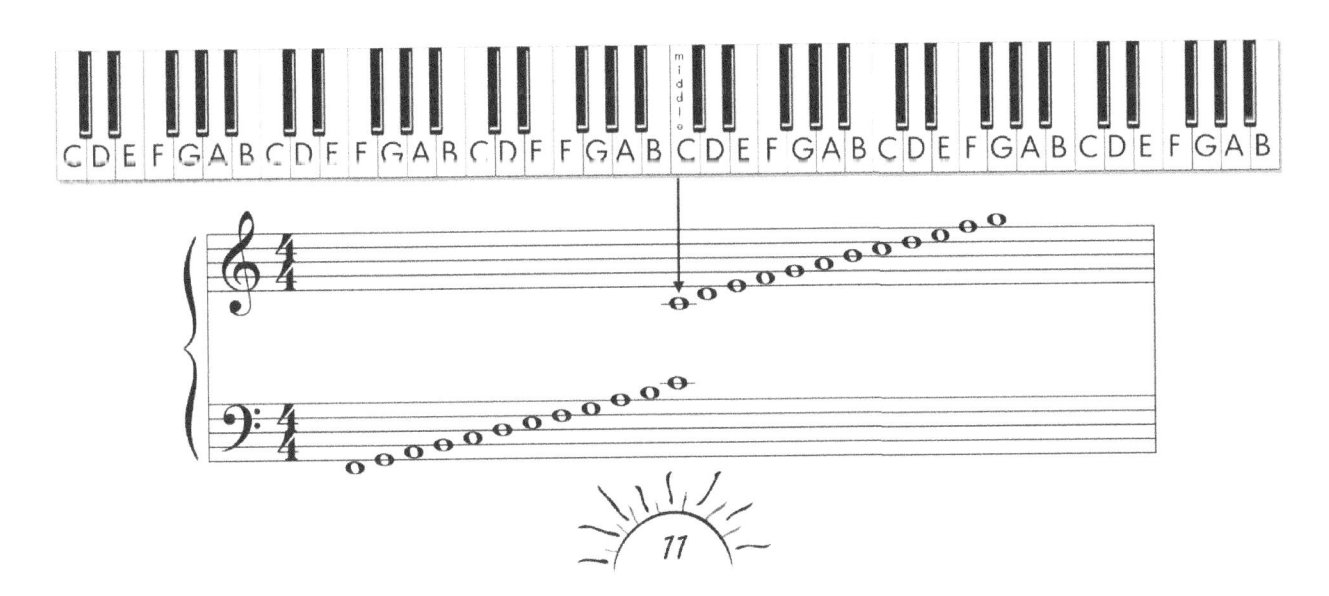

CHAPTER 2

PIECES & STUDIES

STUDY A.1

1- Find the Cs then color them blue
2- Find the Ds then color them purple
3- Find the E then color it red
4- Find the F then color it orange
5- Find the G then color it yellow
6- Find the A then color it pale green

Now you can play all the colored notes on the piano

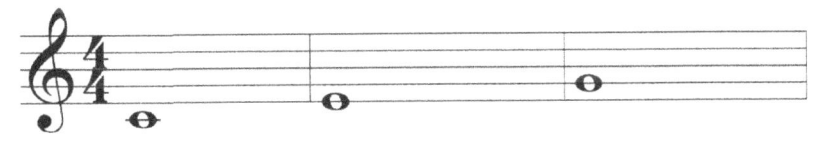

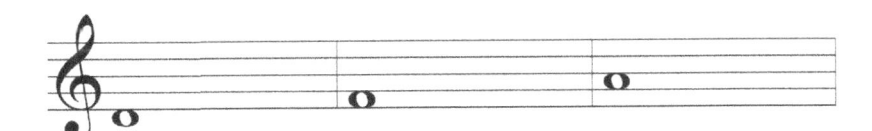

STUDY A.2

Can you write the name of each note in its box?

Continue for the staff below

One more time!?

And now!
Can you play them on the piano?

STUDY A.3

Draw a line from each image to the proper staff

1- Dog goes to the staff that has two whole notes

2- Pig goes to the staff that has four half notes

3- Cat goes to the staff that has quarter notes

4- Kangaroo goes to the staff that has both a whole note and half notes

Now you can play all the staves in order

STUDY A.4

| 1 | 2 | 3 | 4 |
| 5 | 6 | 7 | 8 |

Which measure contains a D? ☐

Which measures are same? ☐ and ☐

Which measures include four quarter notes? ☐ and ☐ and ☐

Can you play the score on piano?

STUDY A.5

What notes are missing on our staff?
Write in the missing notes.

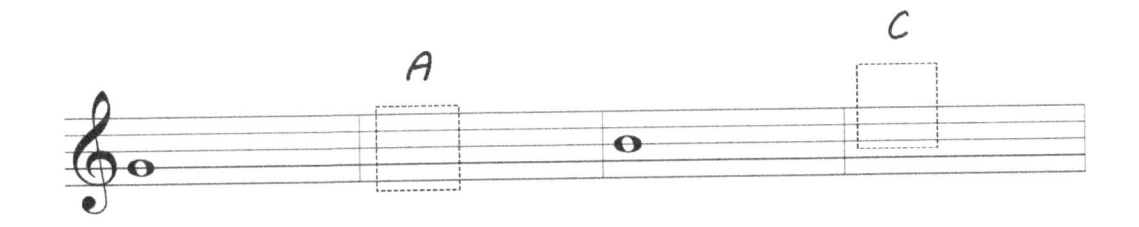

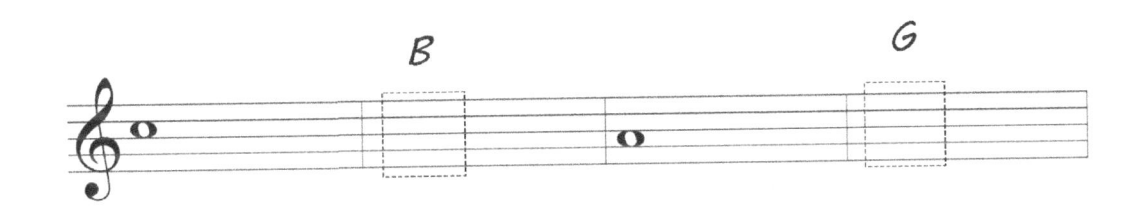

Great job!

Now play all the staves on the piano

LITTLE BO PEEP

C **D**
1   2

Lit - tle Bo Peep has lost her

D   E F G   F E
2   3 4 5   5   4 3

sheep, and does - n't know where_____ to

E   D   G   E
3   2   5   3

find them. Leave them a -

E   F D
     4 2

lone and they will come home,

E F E D C D   C
3 4 3 2 1 2

wag - ging their tails_____ be - hind them.

17

MARY HAD A LITTLE LAMB

E D C D E
3 2 1 2 3

Ma - ry had a lit - tle lamb,

D   E G
2   3 5

lit - tle lamb,   lit - tle lamb.

E D C D E
3 2 1 2 3

Ma - ry had a Lit - tle lamb. Its

D   E D C
2   3 2 1

fleece was white as snow.

18

GIRLS AND BOYS
COME OUT TO PLAY

| G | E | F | D | G | E |
| 5 | 3 | 4 | 2 | 5 | 3 |

Girls and boys, come out to

| C | D | E | F | E | D |
| 1 | 2 | 3 | 4 | 3 | 2 |

play, The moon doth shine____ as

| G | E | C | G | E |
| 5 | 3 | 1 | 5 | 3 |

bright as day. Leave your

| F | D | G | E | C |
| 4 | 2 | 5 | 3 | 1 |

sup - per and leave your sleep,

| D | E | F | E | D | G | E | C |
| 2 | 3 | 4 | 3 | 2 | 5 | 3 | 1 |

come to your play - fel - lows in the street.

LIGHTLY ROW

Lightly row, Lightly row,
O'er the glassy waves we go; Smoothly glide,
smoothly glide, On the silent tide.
Let the winds and waters be,
mingled with our melody; Sing and float,
sing and float, in our little boat.

A-TISKET, A-TASKET

A-tis-ket, A-tas-ket, A green and yel-low bas-ket, I wrote a let-ter to my friend and on the way I dropped it, I dropped it, I dropped it, and on the way I dropped it. A lit-tle boy he picked it up and put it in his poc-ket.

BINGO

This makes every F an F#

There was a farm-er, had a dog, And
Bin - go was his name - o.
B - I - N - G - O,
B - I - N - G - O,
B - I N - G - O, And
Bin - go was his name - o.

TWINKLE TWINKLE LITTLE STAR
(Alphabet Song)

Twin - kle, twin - kle, lit - tle star,

How I won - der what you are!

Up a - bove the clouds so high,

like a dia - mond in the sky.

Twin - kle, twin - kle, lit - tle star,

How I won - der what you are!

HICKORY DICKORY DOCK

Hick - o - ry dick - o - ry

dock! The mouse ran

up the clock. The

clock struck one, the mouse ran down.

Hick - o - ry dick - o - ry dock.

Thumb cross over, like here, is when you crossing another finger over your thumb.

TEN LITTLE INDIANS

One lit-tle, two lit-tle, three lit-tle In-di-ans,

four lit-tle, five lit-tle, six lit-tle In-di-ans,

seven lit-tle, eight lit-tle, nine lit-tle In-di-ans,

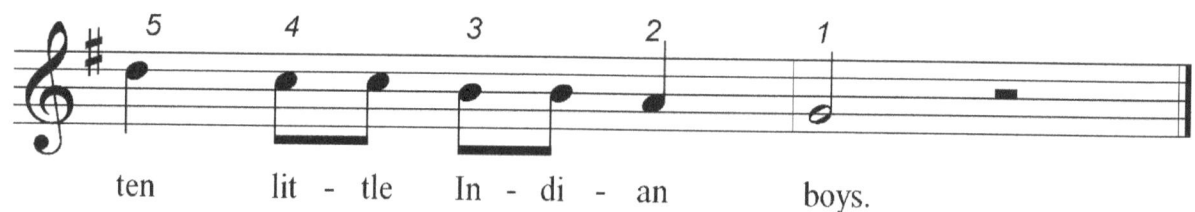

ten lit-tle In-di-an boys.

YANKEE DOODLE

Yan - kee Doo - dle went to town,

rid - ing on a po - ny,

stuck a fea - ther in his cap and

called it Ma - ca - ro - ni.

THE MUFFIN MAN

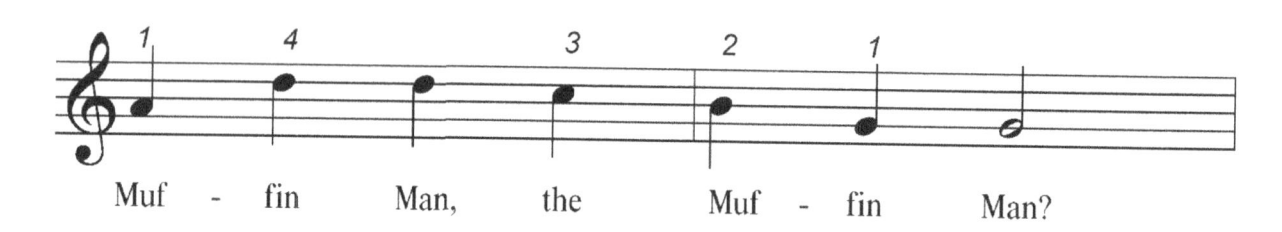

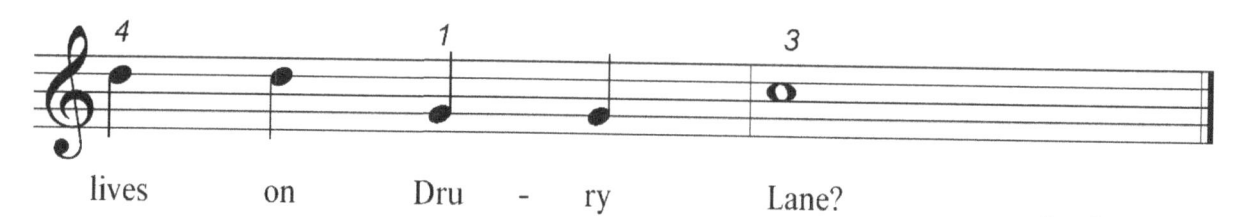

Do you know the Muf - fin Man, the Muf - fin Man, the Muf - fin Man?

Do you know the Muf - fin Man who lives on Dru - ry Lane?

27

NEW WORLD
by Antonín Dvorák

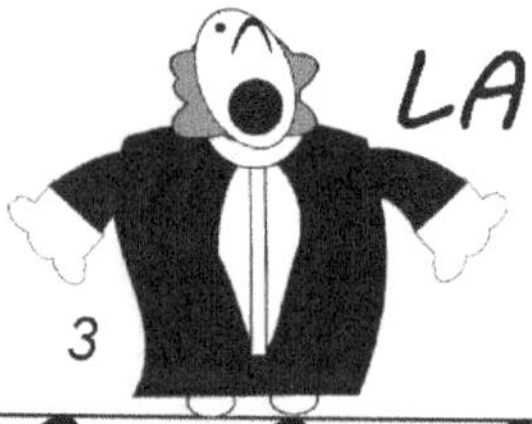

LA DONNA È MOBILE

by Giuseppe Verdi

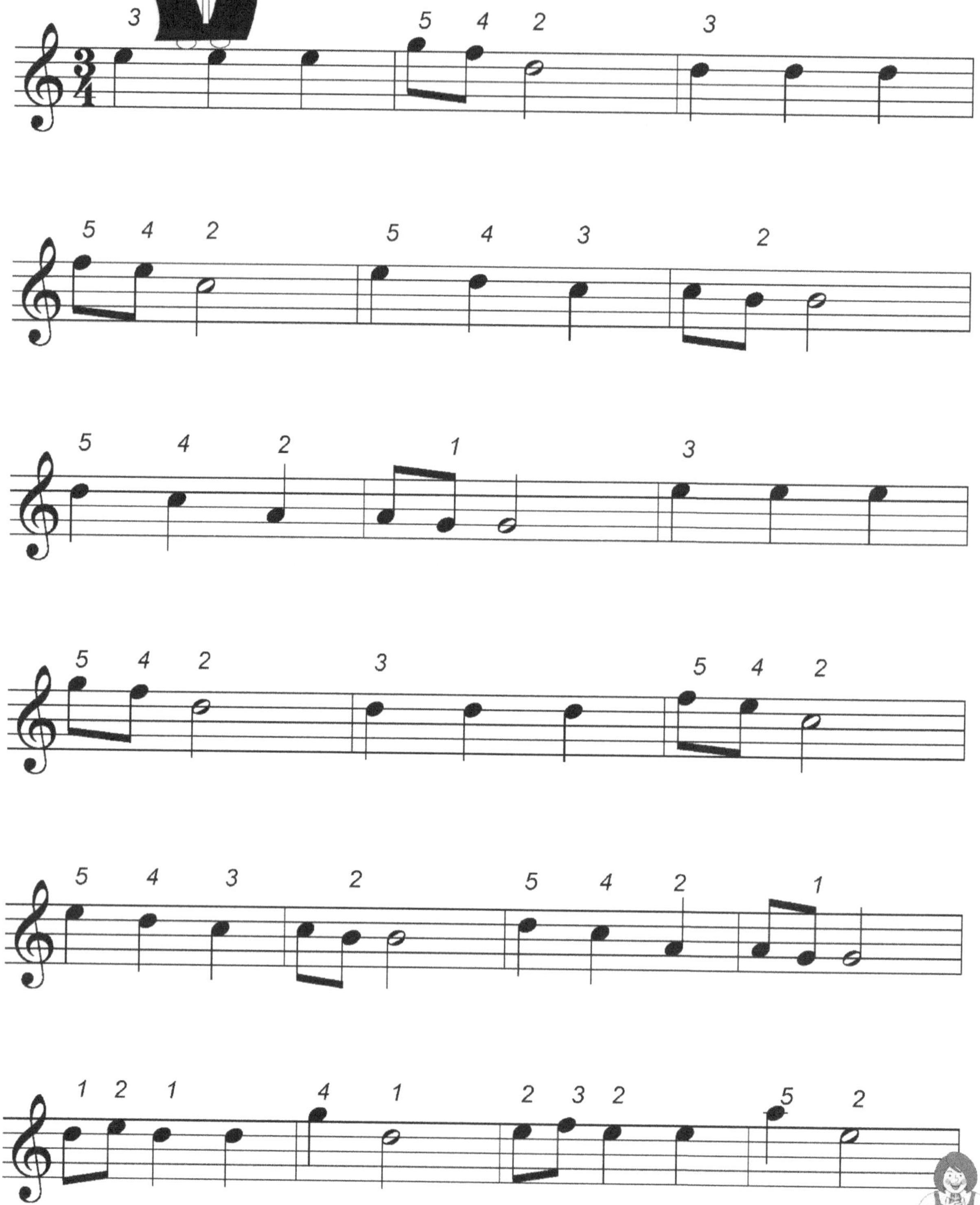

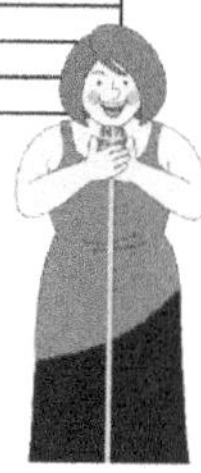

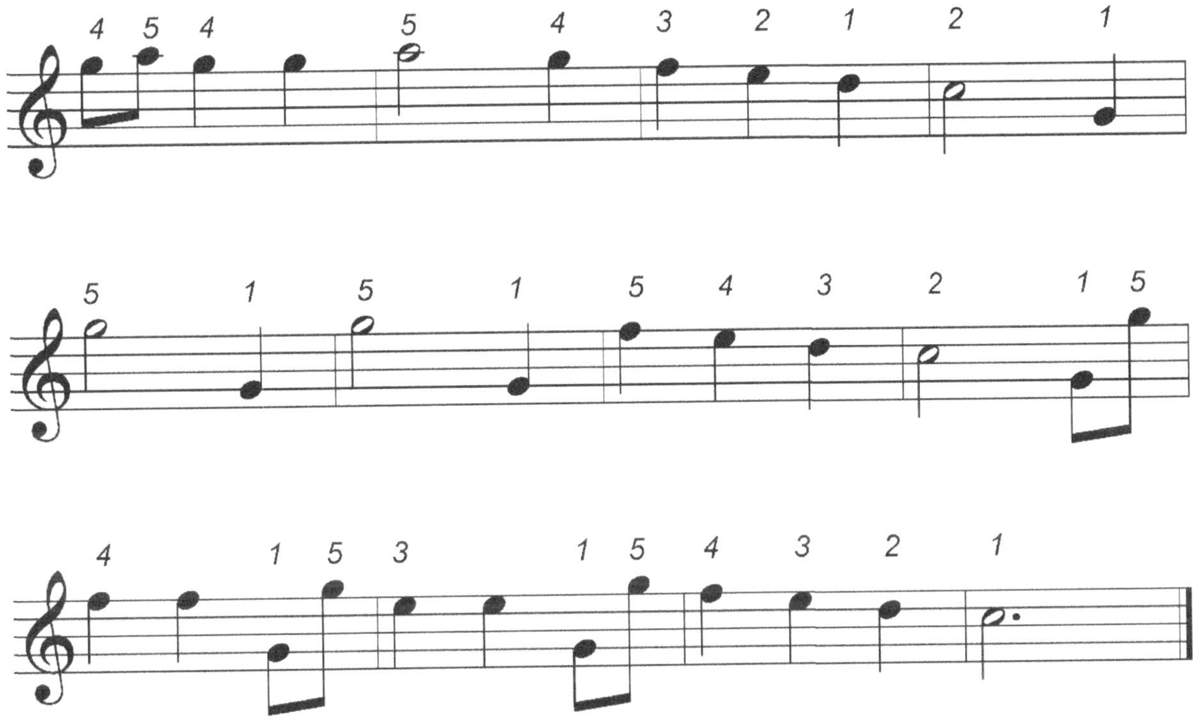
4 5 4 5 4 3 2 1 2 1
5 1 5 1 5 4 3 2 1 5
4 1 5 3 1 5 4 3 2 1

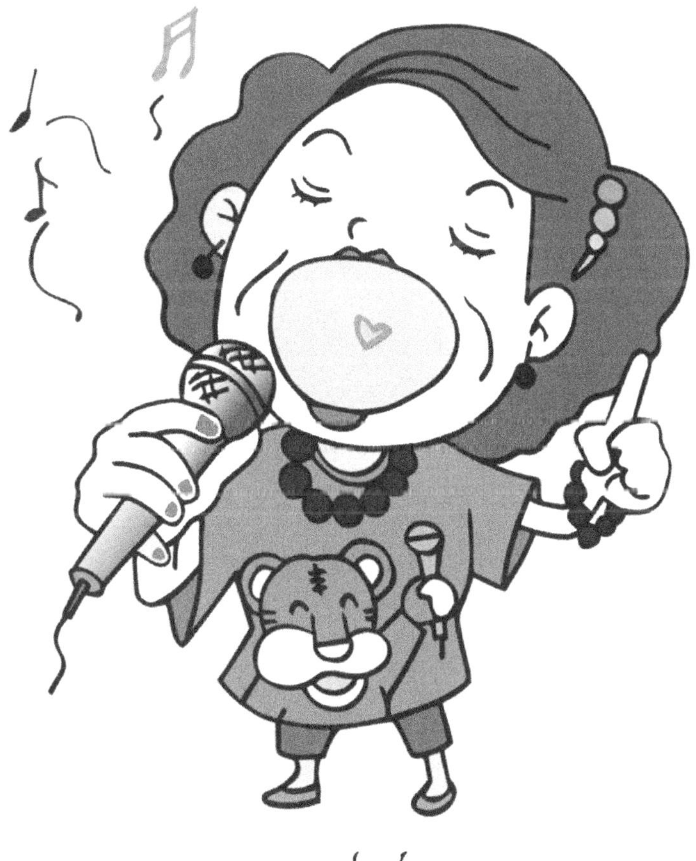

O MIO BABBINO CARO

This makes every B a Bb

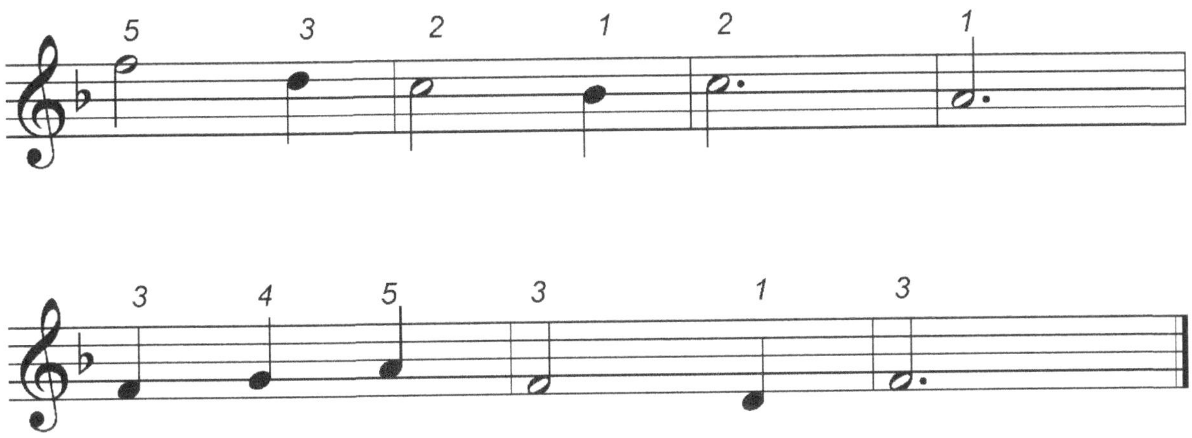
5 3 2 1 2 1
3 4 5 3 1 3

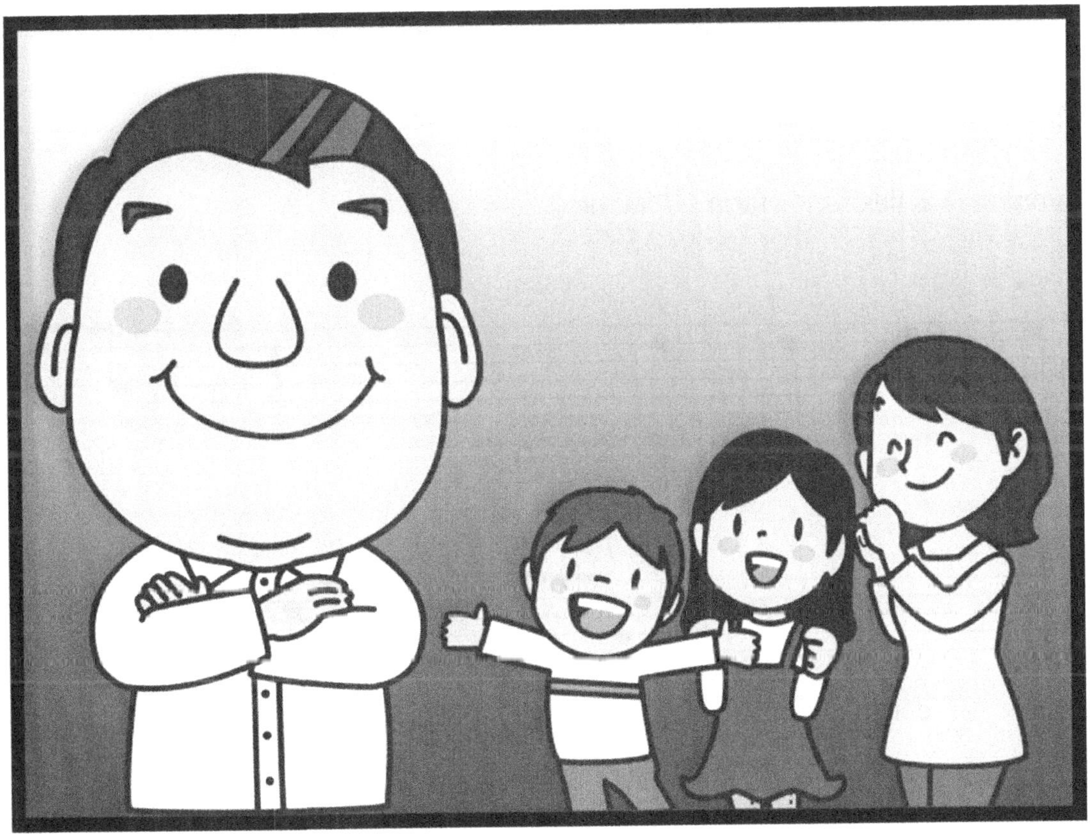

OLD MACDONALD HAD A FARM

Old Mac - Do - nald had a farm,

E - I - E - I - O And

on this farm he had a chick.

E - I - E - I - O With a

chick - chick here and a chick chick there.

Here a chick, there a chick, e - very-where a chick chick

Old Mac - Do - nald had a farm.

E - I - E - I - O

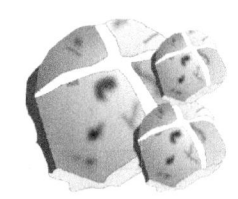

HOT CROSS BUNS

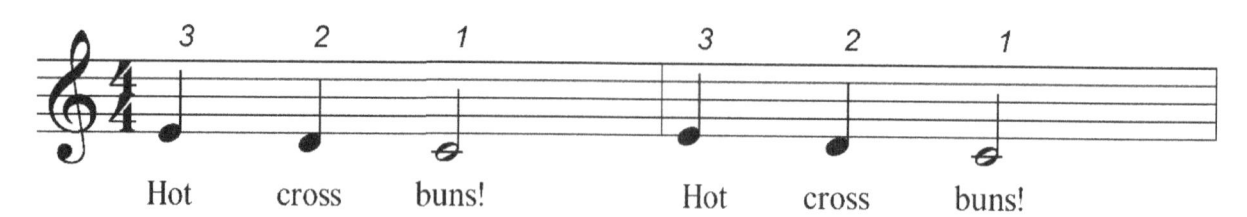

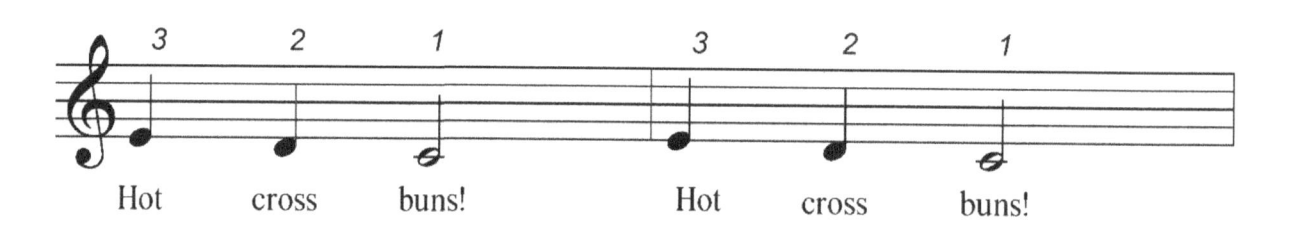

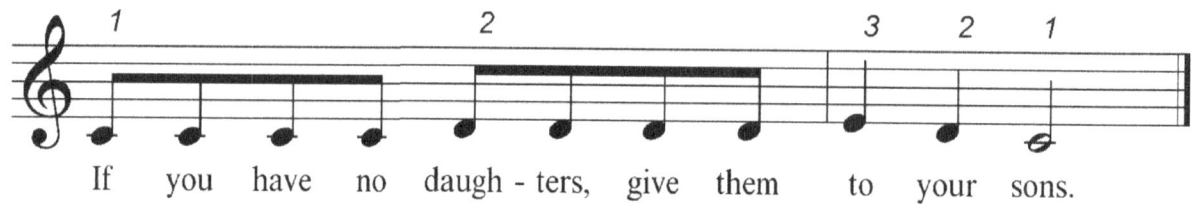

Hot cross buns! Hot cross buns!

One a penny, Two a penny, Hot cross buns,

Hot cross buns! Hot cross buns!

If you have no daugh-ters, give them to your sons.

PEASE PORRIDGE

Pease por-ridge hot, pease por-ridge cold,

pease por-ridge in the pot, nine days old.

Some like it hot, some like it cold,

some like it in the pot, nine days old.

THE STORM
by Ludwig Van Beethoven

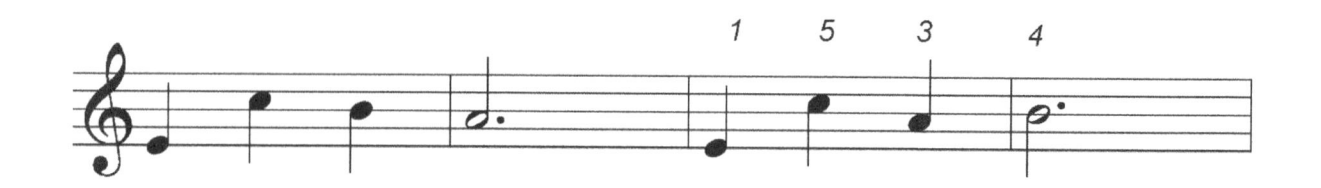

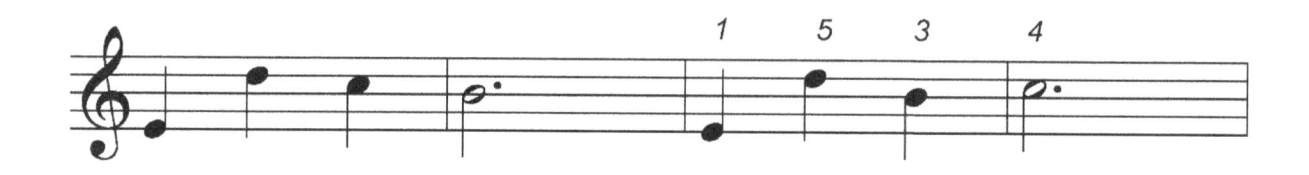

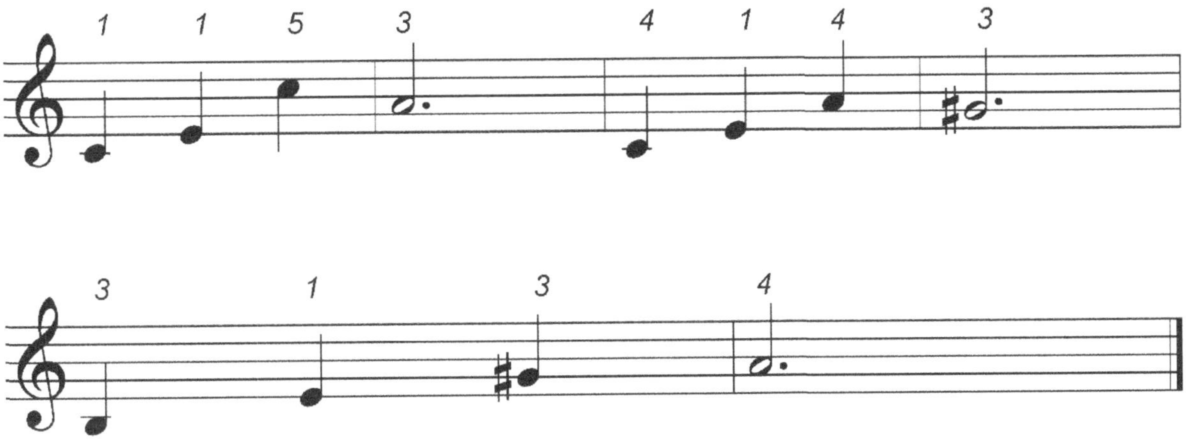
1 1 5 3 4 1 4 3
3 1 3 4

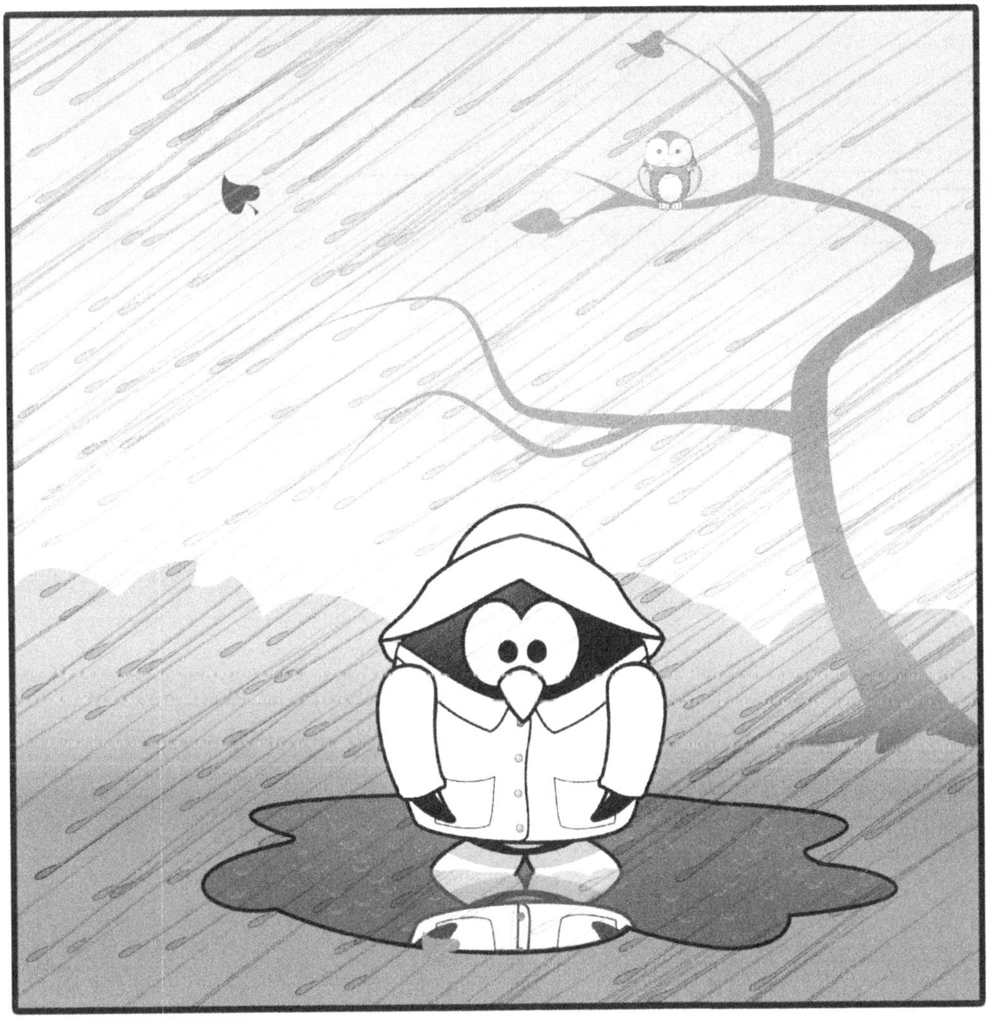

THE BLUE DANUBE
by Johann Strauss

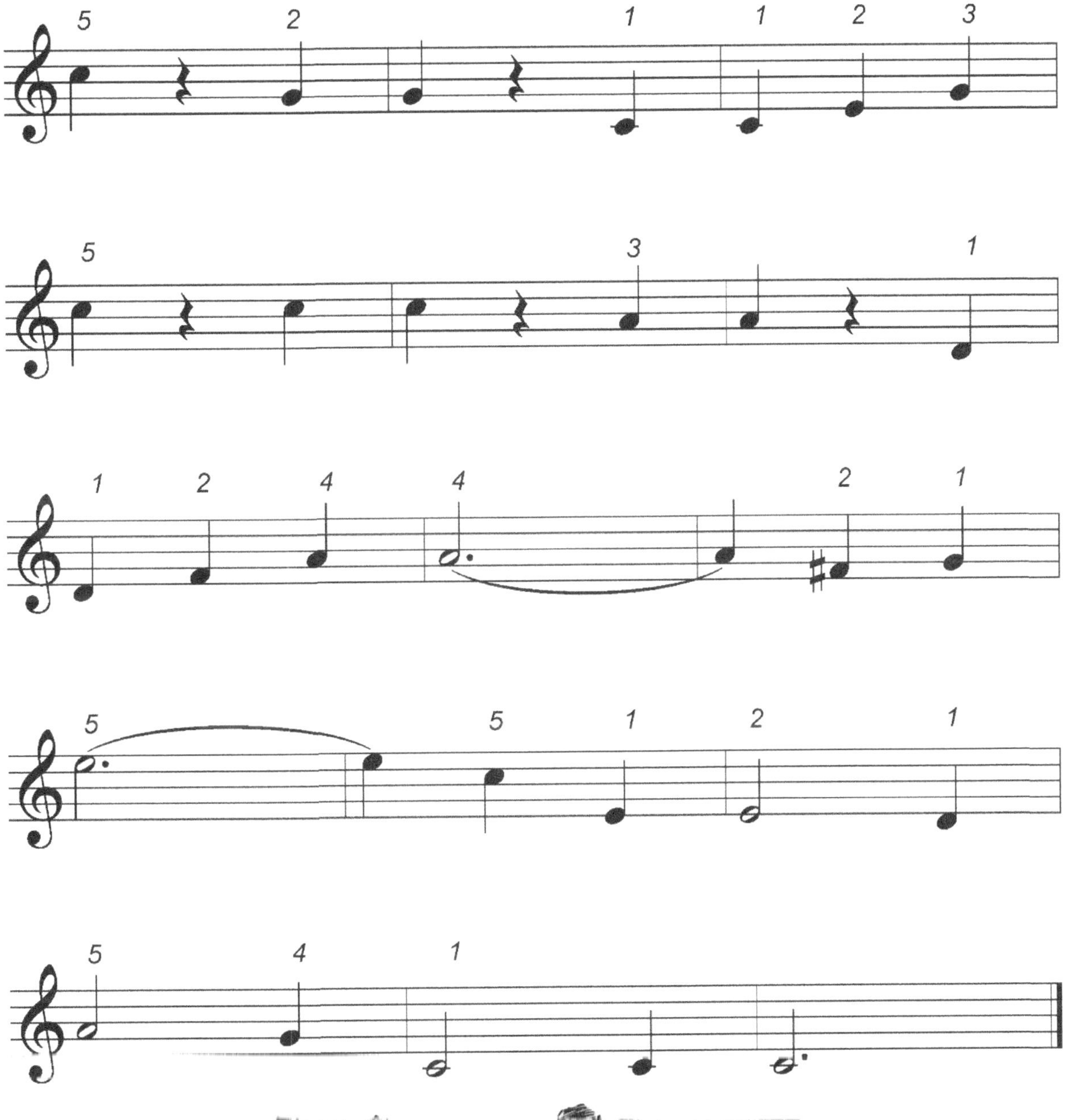

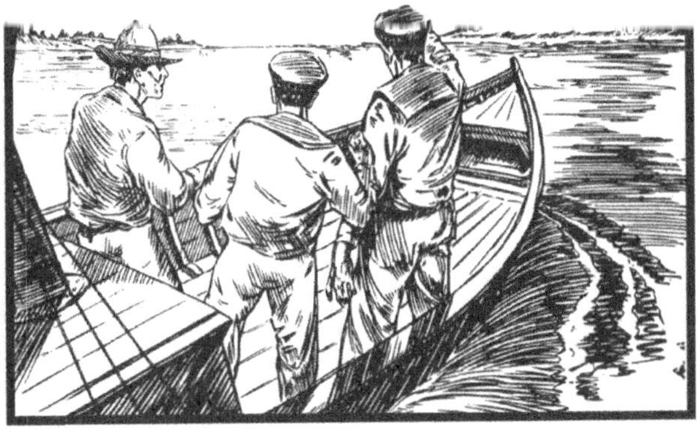

STUDY B.1

1- Find the Cs then color them blue   2- Find the Ds then color them purple

3- Find the Es then color them red   4- Find the Fs then color them orange

5- Find the Gs then color them yellow   6- Find the A then color it pale green

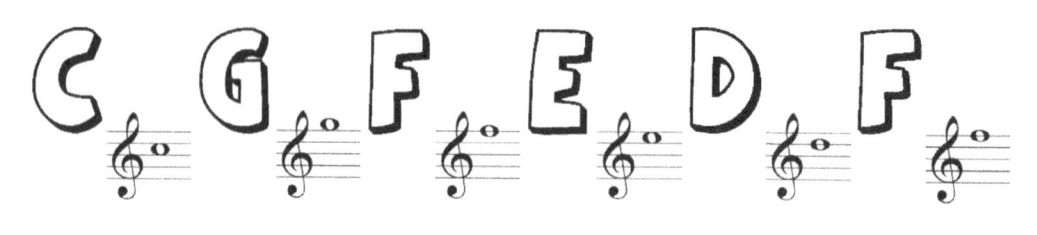

C G F E D F

E G A E D F

C E C

Now you can play all the colored notes on the piano

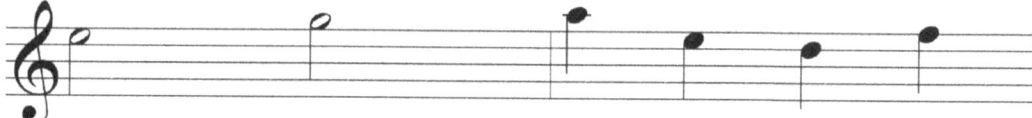

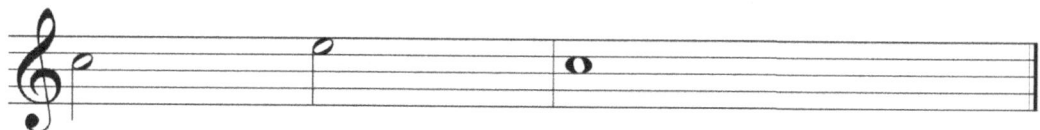

STUDY B.2

Can you write the name of each note in its box?

Continue for the staff below

One more time!?

And now!
Can you play them on the piano?

STUDY B.3

Draw a line from each image to the proper staff

1- Pencil goes to the staff that has two half notes
2- Sharpener goes to the staff that finishes on G
3- Eraser goes to the staff that has four Ds
4- Book goes to the staff that finishes on C

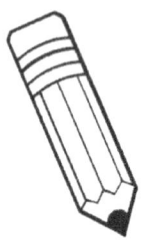

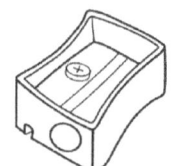

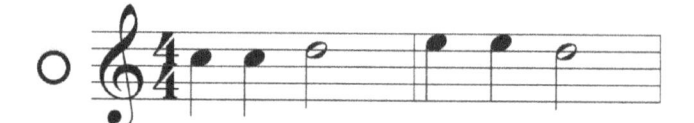

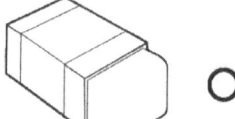

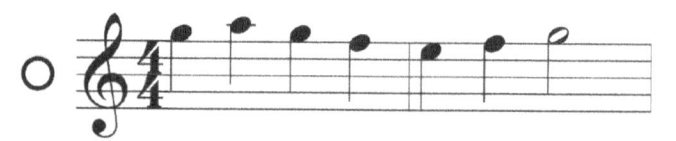

Now you can play all the staves in order

STUDY B.4

[1] [2] [3] [4]

[5] [6] [7] [8]

Which measure contains two Ds? ☐

Which measures include a whole note? ☐ and ☐

Which measures begin with C? ☐ and ☐ and ☐

Can you play the score on piano?

STUDY B.5

What notes are missing on our staff?
Write in the missing notes.

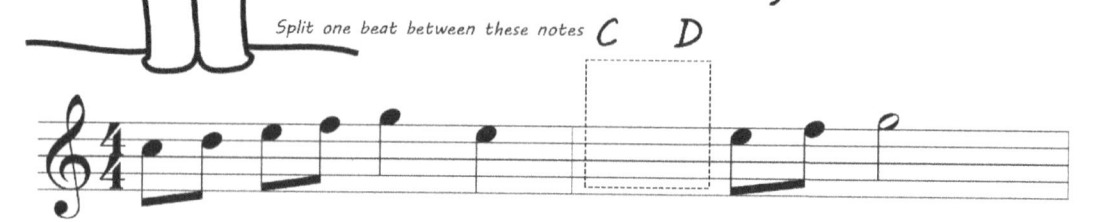

Split one beat between these notes C D

E

Split one beat between these notes
E D

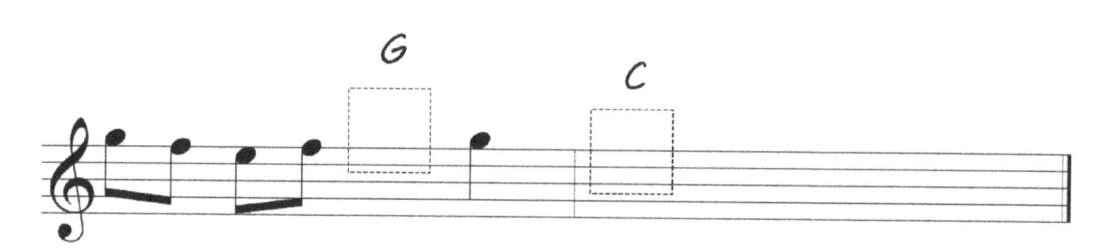

E

G

C

Great job!

Now play all the staves on the piano

ALOHA OE

Fare - well, my love, fare - well to thee, while you're a - way I'll pray for your re - turn - ing. One fond em - brace, one kiss and then, fare - well, un - til we meet a - gain.

FÜR ELISE
by Ludwig Van Beethoven

CAN-CAN

Sometimes, like here, you need to change fingers on repeated notes to be prepared for next notes.

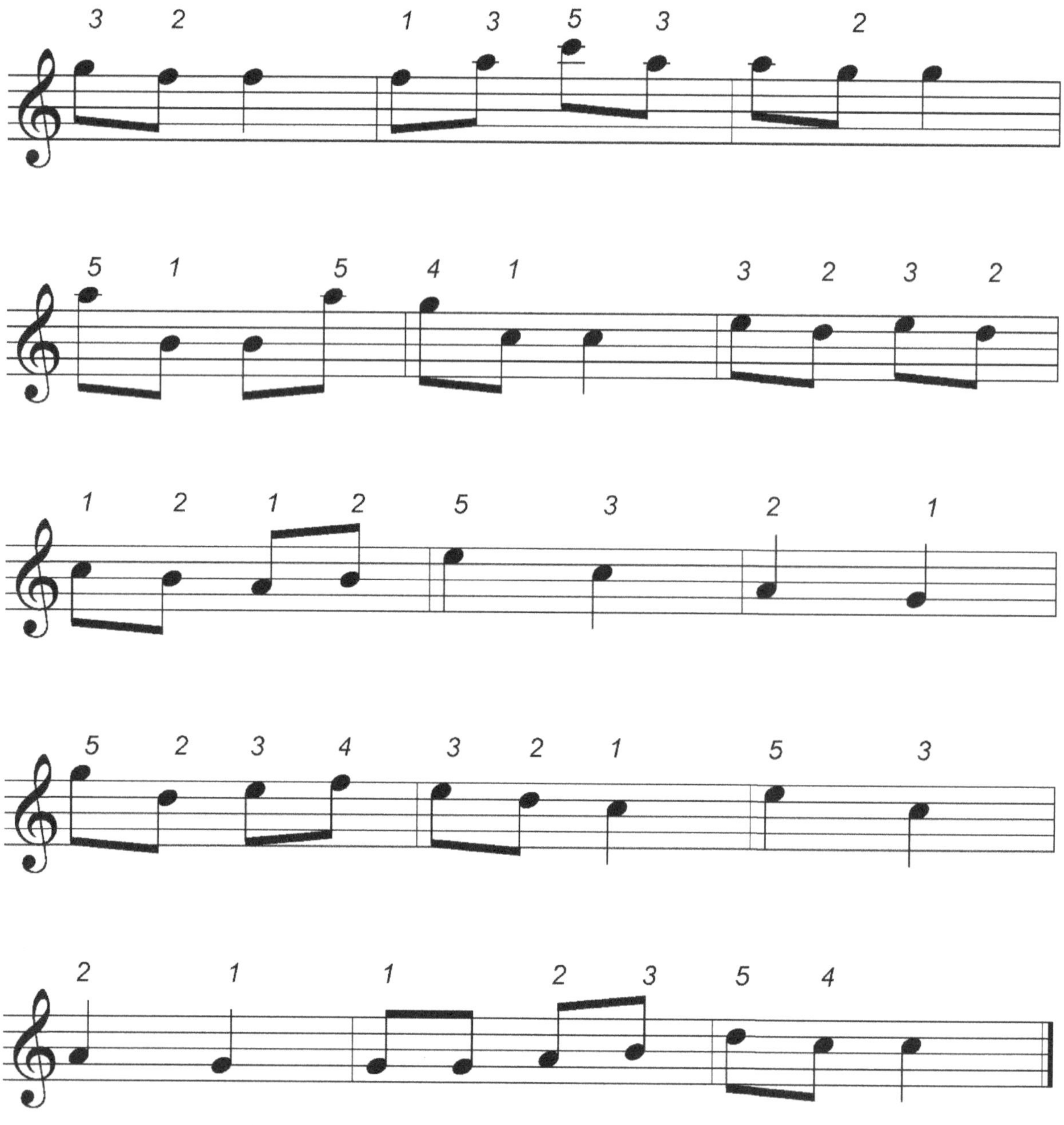

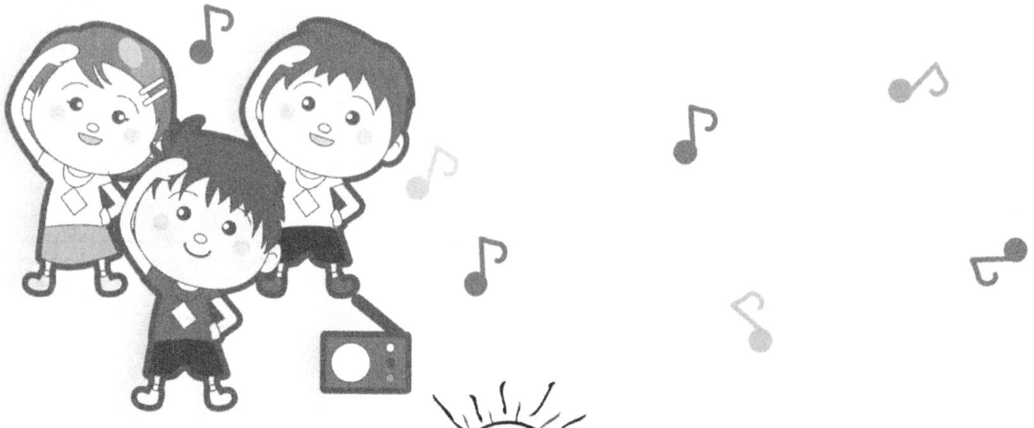

SHE'LL BE COMING
ROUND THE MOUNTAIN

She'll be com-ing round the moun-tain when she comes, _____ She'll be com-ing round the moun-tain when she comes, _____ She'll be com-ing round the moun-tain, She'll be com-ing round the moun-tain, She'll be com-ing round the moun-tain when she comes. _____

CLAIR DE LUNE
by Gabriel Fauré

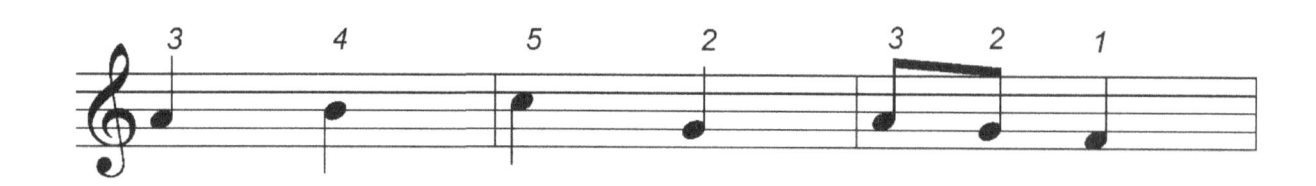

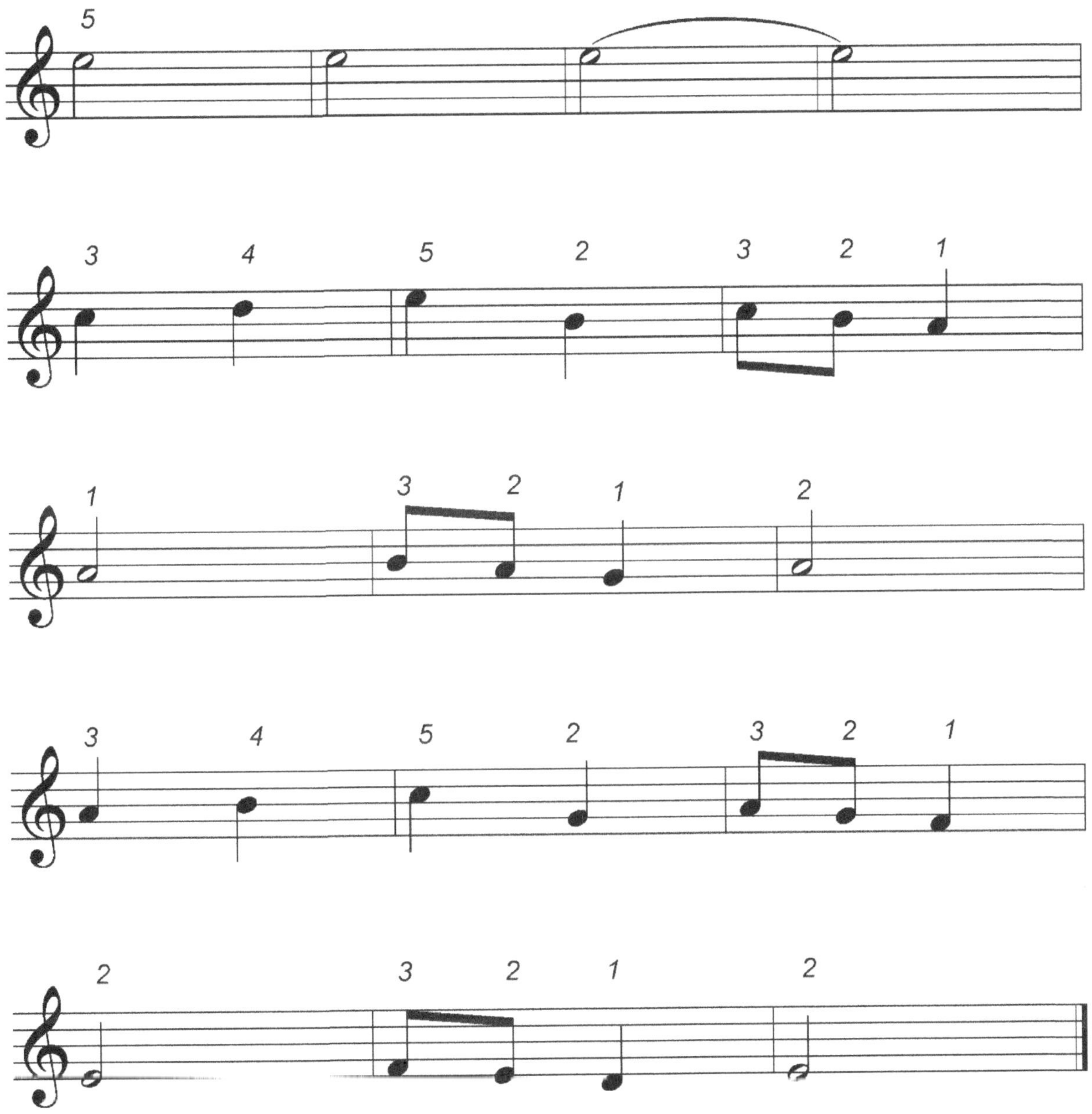

POMP AND CIRCUMSTANCE
by Edward Elgar

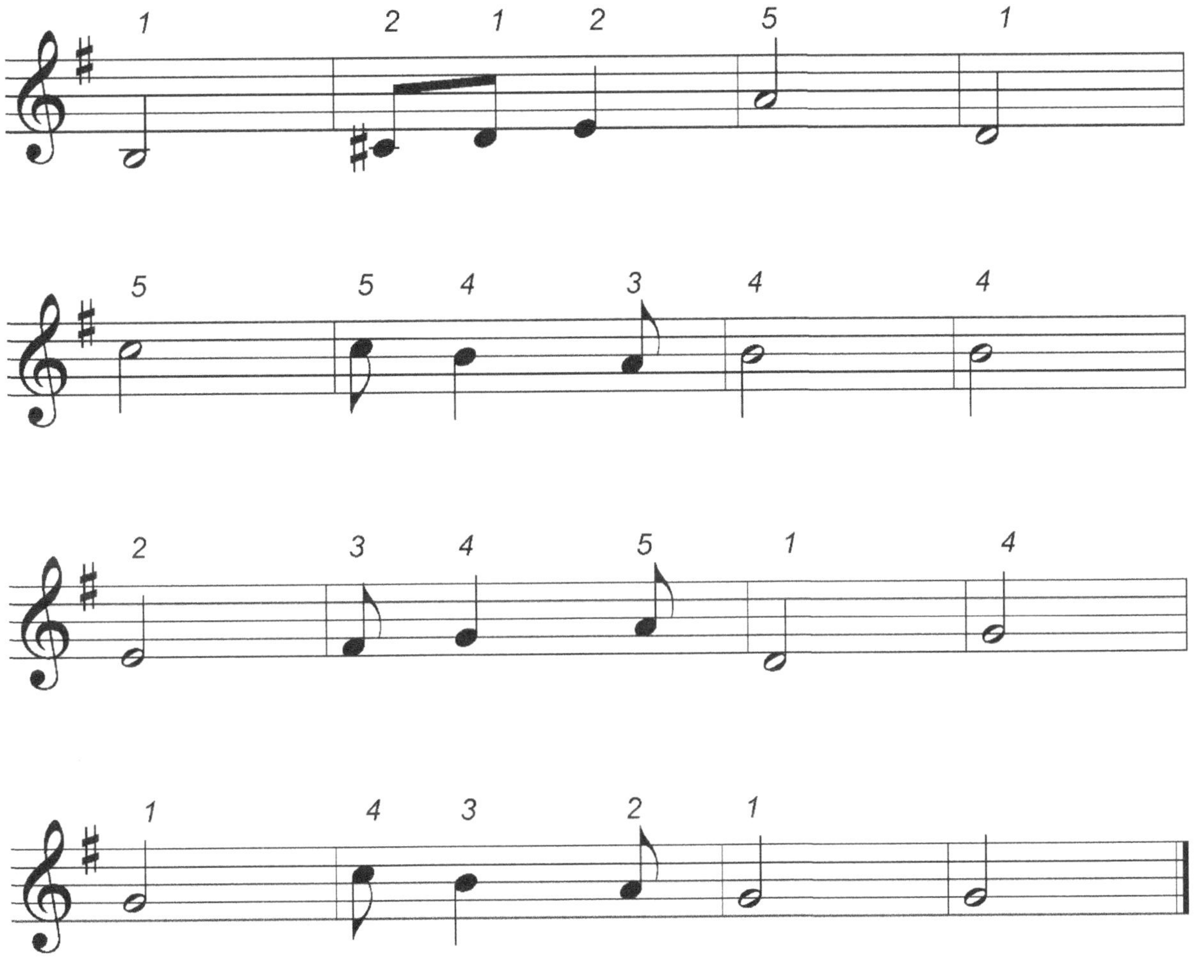

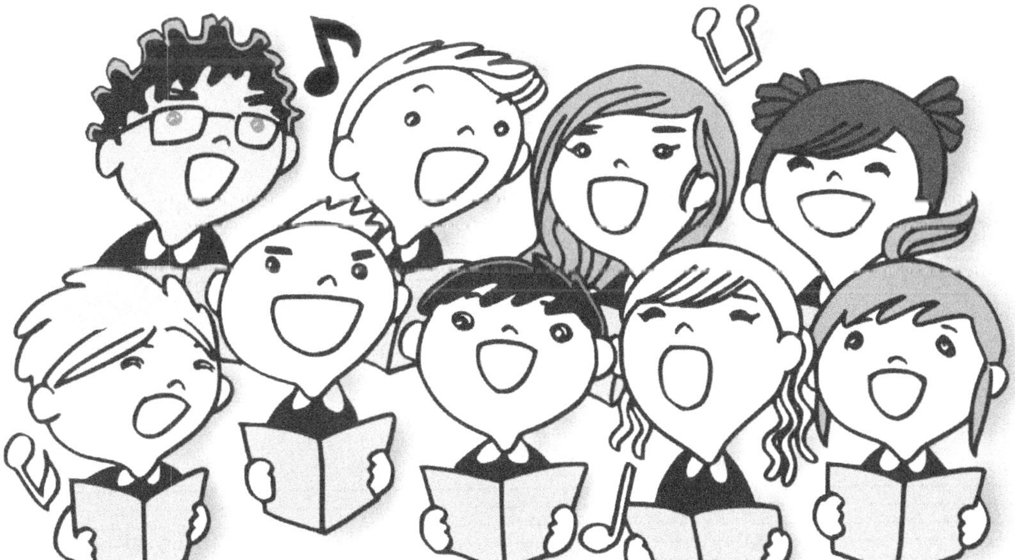

DON GIOVANNI
by W. A. Mozart

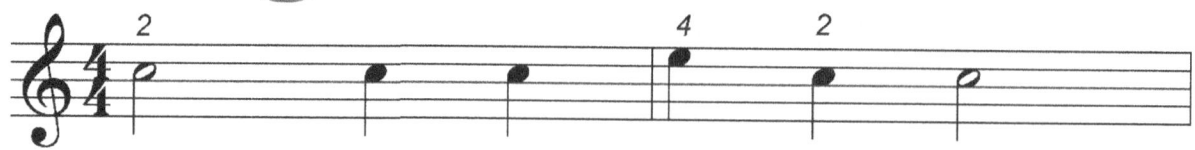

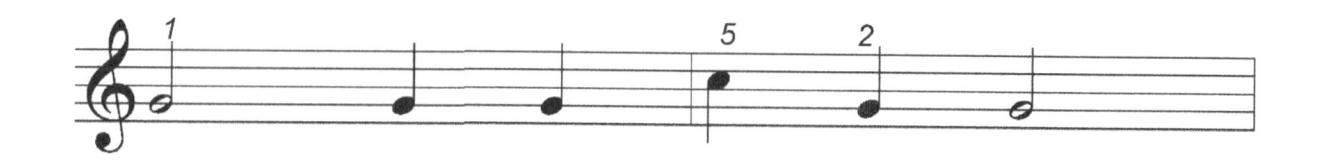

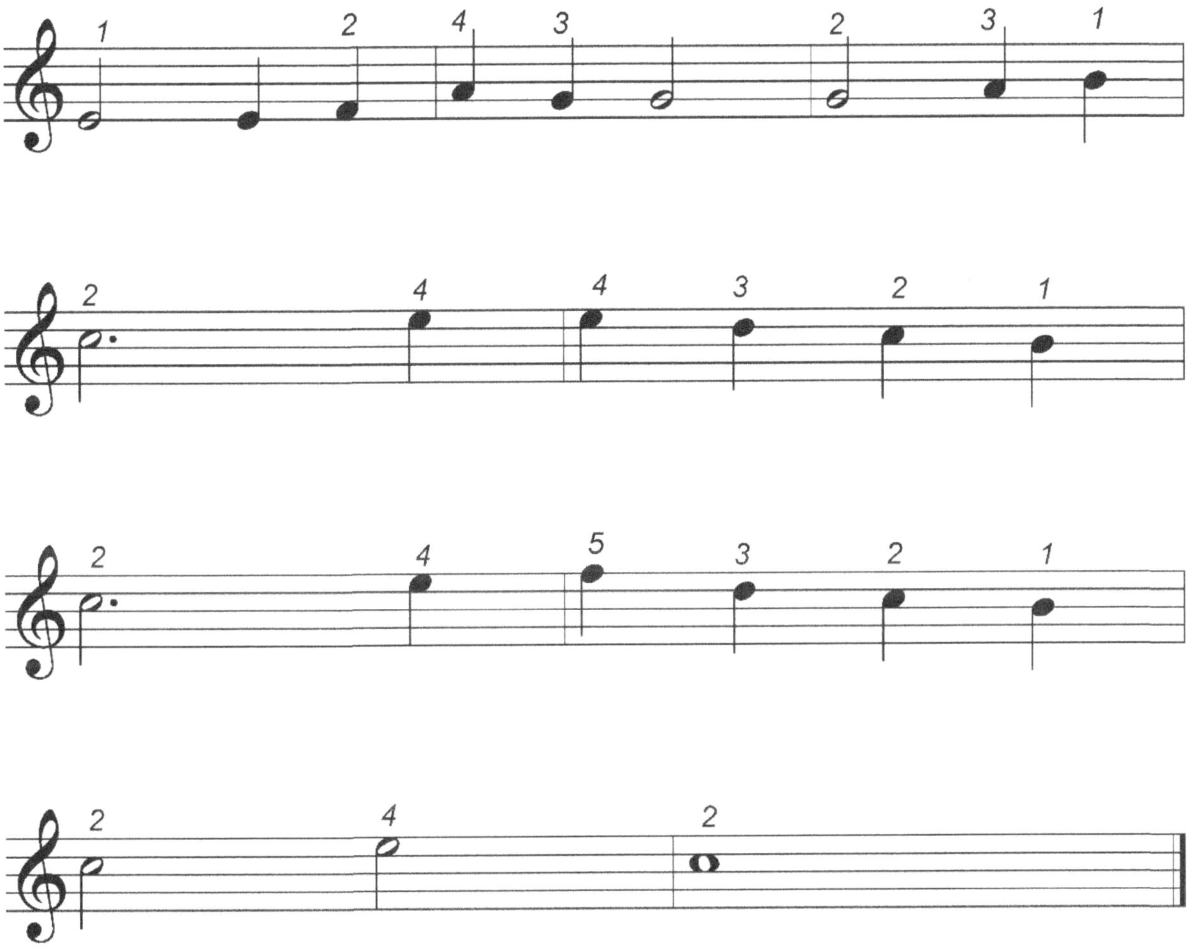

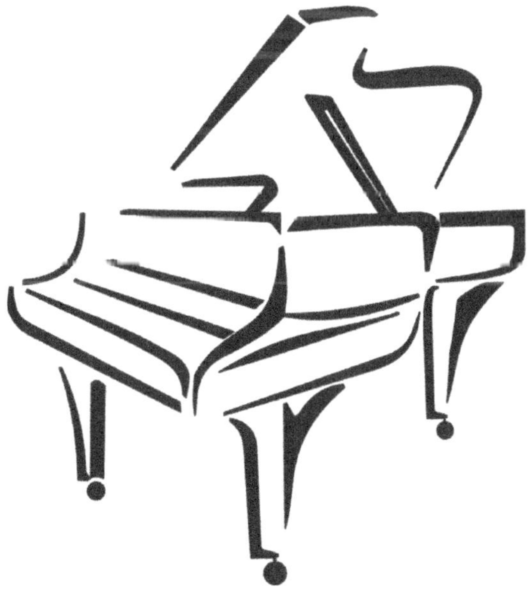

HEAD, SHOULDERS, KNEES AND TOES

Heads shoul-ders knees and toes knees and toes

Heads shoul-ders knees and toes knees and toes___ and___

eyes and ears and mouth___ and___ nose

Heads shoul-ders knees and toes knees and toes.

57

IF YOU'RE HAPPY AND YOU KNOW IT

If you're hap-py and you know it, clap your hands. If you're hap-py and you know it, clap your hands. If you're hap-py and you know it, and you real-ly want to show it, if you're hap-py and you know it, clap your hands.

LULLABY
by Johannes Brahms

CAMPTOWN RACES

Camp-town la-dies sing this song, doo-dah,

doo-dah. Camp-town race-track five miles long,

oh, doo-dah day. Goin' to run all

night! Goin' to run all day!

Camp-town race-track five miles long, oh, doo-dah day.

60

ODE TO JOY
by Ludwig Van Beethoven

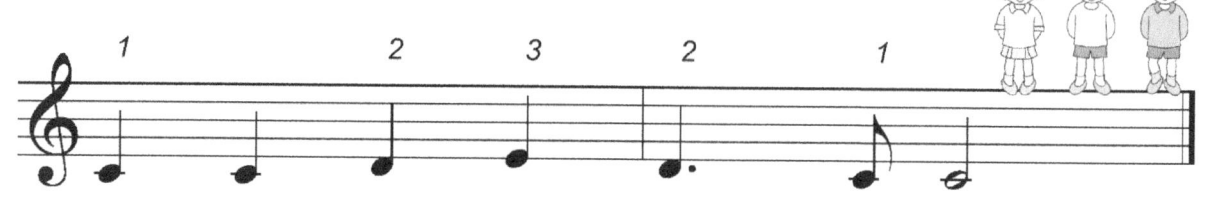

JINGLE BELLS

Jin - gle bells, Jin - gle bells, Jin - gle all the way,

Oh what fun it is to ride in a one horse o - pen sleigh, hey!

Jin - gle bells, Jin - gle bells, Jin - gle all the way,

Oh what fun it is to ride in a one horse o - pen sleigh.

ROCK-A-BYE BABY

Rock - a - bye ba - by on the tree - top, When the wind blows, the cra - dle will rock, When the bough breaks, the cra - dle will fall, and down will come ba - by, cra - dle and all.

AMERICA THE BEAUTIFUL

Oh, beau - ti - ful for spa - cious skies, For am - ber waves of grain. For pur - ple moun - tain ma - jes - ties A - bove the frui - ted plain! A - me - ri - ca! A - me - ri - ca! God shed his grace on thee, And crown thy good with bro - ther - hood, From sea to shi - ning sea!

GREENSLEEVES

Al - as my love y-ou do me wrong t-o cast me off di-s-cour-teous-ly and I have loved y-ou oh so long d-e-li-gh-ting in yo-ur com-pany Green-sleeves wa-s my de-light, G-reen-sleeves my heart o-f go-ld

Green - sleeves was my heart of joy a - nd who but my la - d - y Green - sleeves

AURA LEE

As the black-bird in the spring, Neath the will-low tree,

Sat and piped I heard him sing, Sing of Au - ra Lee.

Au - ra Lee, Au - ra Lee, maid of gold - en hair.

Sun-shine come a - long with thee, and swal-lows in the air.

AMAZING GRACE

A - ma - zing grace, how sweet the sound that saved a wretch like me. I once was lost, but now am found, was blind, but now I see.

THE WHEELS ON THE BUS

The wheels on the bus go round and round, round and round, round and round, The wheels on the bus go round and round, All through the town.

SWAN LAKE
Pyotr Ilyich Tchaikovsky

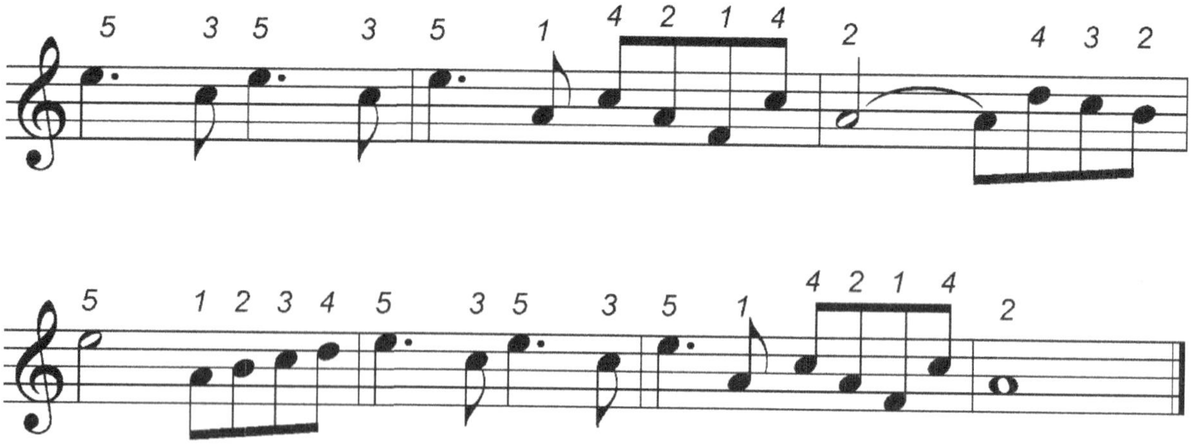
5 3 5 3 5 1 4 2 1 4 2 4 3 2
5 1 2 3 4 5 3 5 3 5 1 4 2 1 4 2

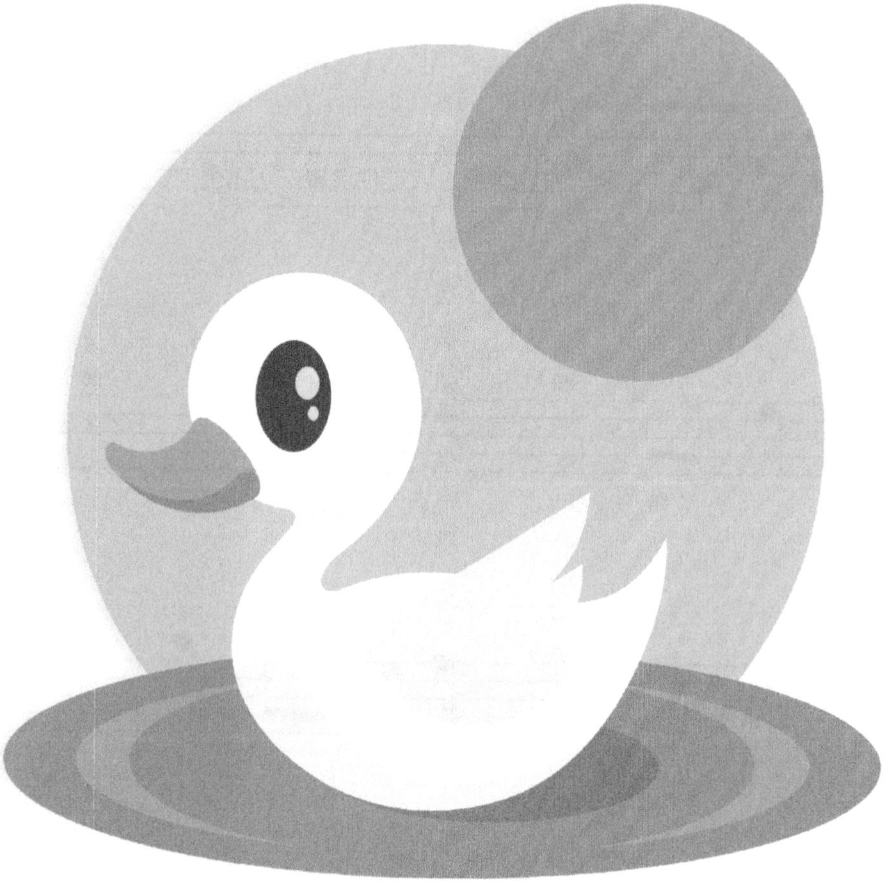

STUDY C.1

1- Find the Cs then color them blue

2- Find the D then color it purple

3- Find the E then color it red

4- Find the F then color it orange

5- Find the G then color it yellow

6- Find the A then color it pale green

7- Find the B then color it dark green

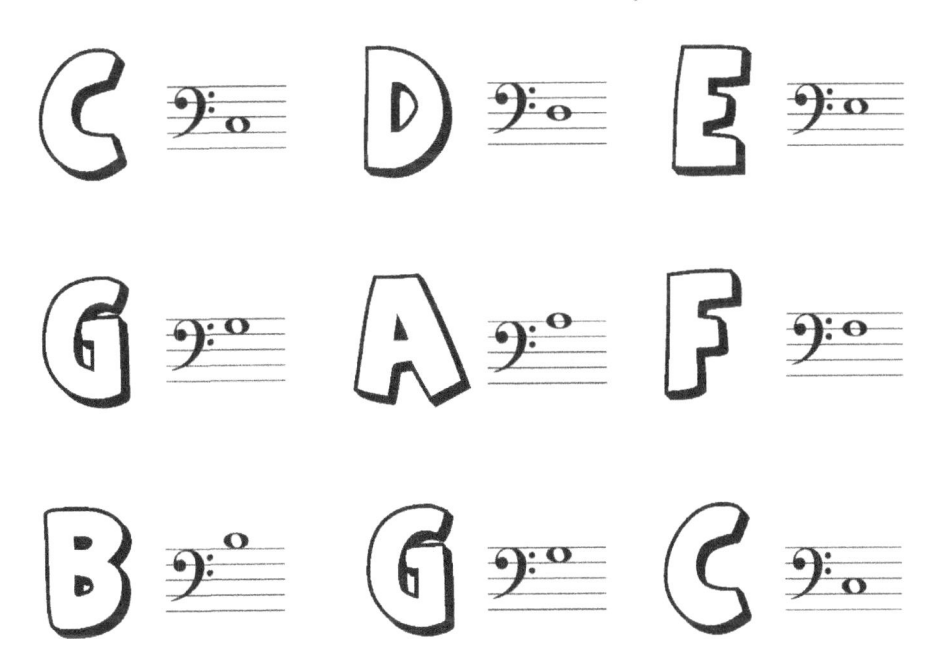

C D E

G A F

B G C

Now you can play all the colored note on piano

STUDY C.2

Can you write the name of each note in its box?

Continue for the staff below

One more time!?

And now!
Can you play them on the piano?

STUDY C.3

Draw a line from each image to the proper staff

1- Sun goes to the staff with only quarter notes
2- Cloud goes to the staff that starts with G
3- Moon goes to the staff that has two half notes
4- Star goes to the staff that finishes on C

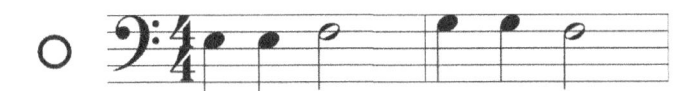

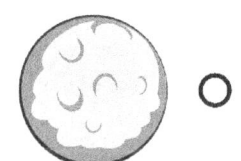

Now you can play all the staves in order

STUDY C.4

Which measure finishes on E?

Which measures include an eighth note?
☐ and ☐

Which measure have the same rhythm?
☐ and ☐ and ☐

Can you play the score on piano?

STUDY C.S

What notes are missing on our staff?
Write in the missing notes.

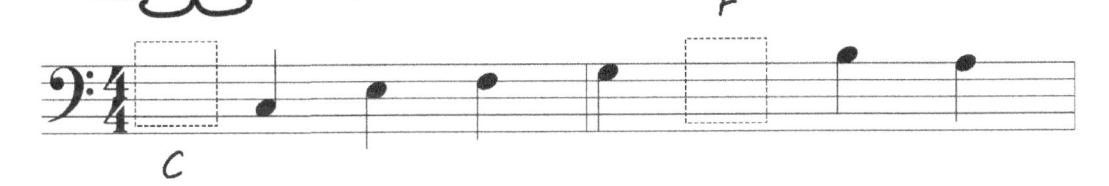

Great job!

Now play all the staves on the piano

BIG BEN

Bass Clef
Play with left hand

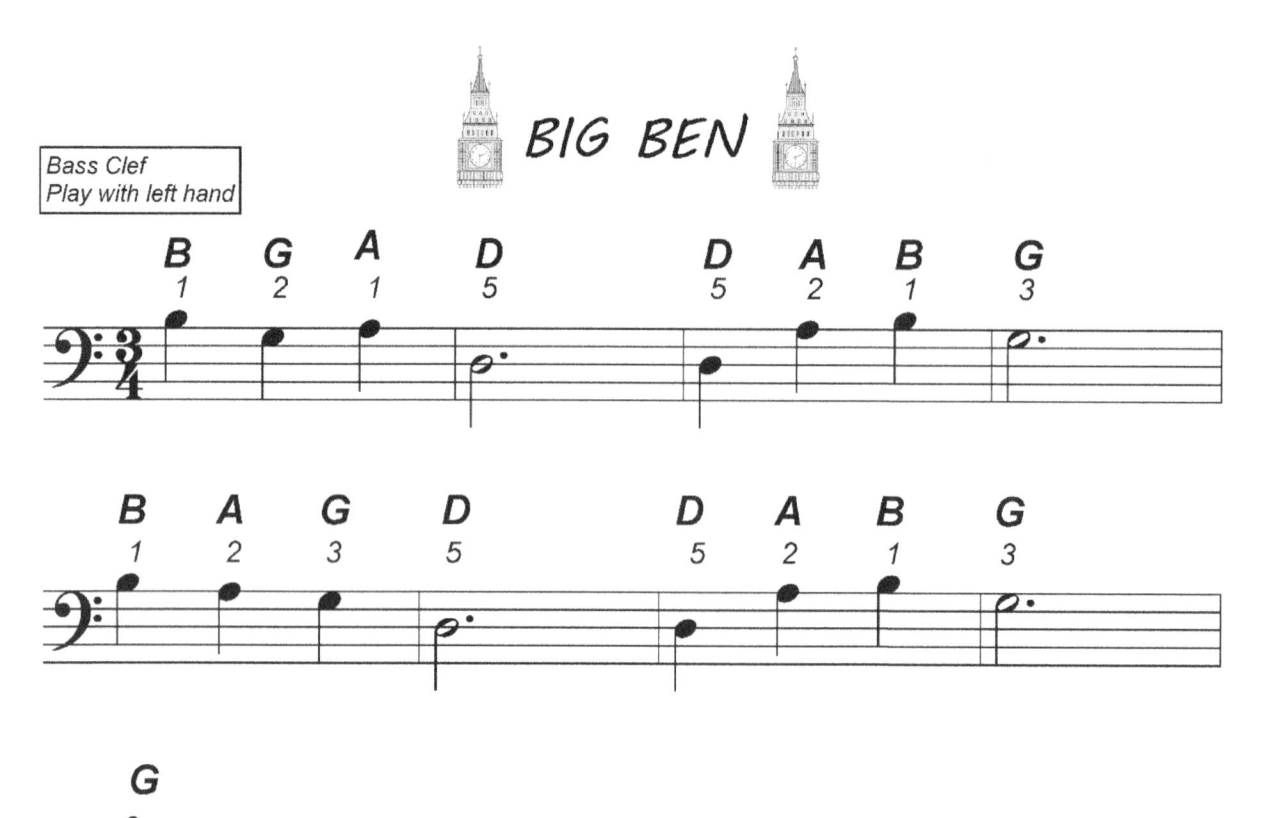

| B | G | A | D | D | A | B | G |
| 1 | 2 | 1 | 5 | 5 | 2 | 1 | 3 |

| B | A | G | D | D | A | B | G |
| 1 | 2 | 3 | 5 | 5 | 2 | 1 | 3 |

G
3

JACK AND JILL

C **D** **E** **F**
5   4   3   2

Jack and Jill want up the hill to

G **A** **B** **C**
1   3   2   1.

fetch a pail of wa - ter.

C **B** **A** **G**
1   2   3   1

Jack fell down and broke his crown and

F **E** **D** **C**
2   3   4   5

Jill came tumb - ling af - ter.

I'M A LITTLE TEAPOT

I'm a lit - tle tea - pot, short and stout. Here is my han - dle, here is my spout. When I get all steamed up, hear me shout: "Tip me o - ver and pour me out."

79

SAKURA

ROW, ROW, ROW YOUR BOAT

Row, row, row your boat,

Gen - tly down the stream.

Mer - ri - ly, mer - ri - ly, mer - ri - ly, mer - ri - ly.

Life is but a dream.

LOOBY LOO

Here we go loo - by loo,_____

Here we go loo - by light._____

Here we go loo - by loo,_____

all on a Sat - ur - day night._____

HUMPTY DUMPTY

Hump - ty Dump - ty sat on a wall, Hump - ty Dump - ty had a great fall, All the king's hor - ses and all the king's men could - n't put Hump - ty to - ge - ther a - gain.

STUDY D.1

1- Find the Cs then color them blue

2- Find the D then color it purple

3- Find the Es then color them red

4- Find the A then color it orange

5- Find the Gs then color them yellow

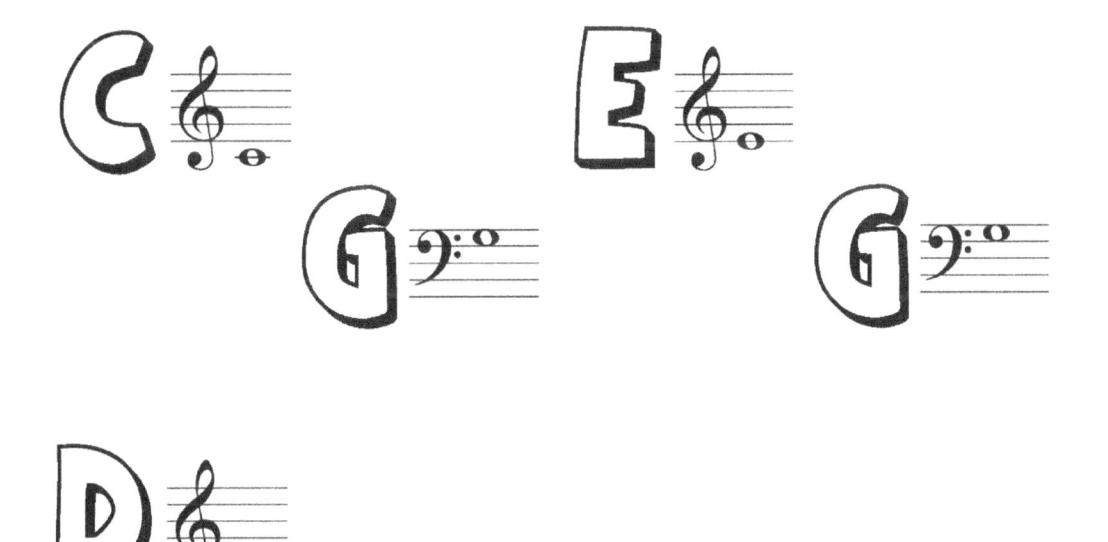

Now you can play all the colored notes on piano

STUDY D.2

Can you write the name of each note in its box?

Continue for the staff below

And now!
Can you play them on the piano?

STUDY D.3

Draw a line from each image to the proper staff

1- Airplane goes to the staff with only C

2- Car goes to the staff that starts with D

3- Locomotive goes to the staff that has two Es

4- Bicycle goes to the staff that has a G

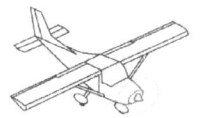

Now you can play all the staves in order

STUDY D.4

Which measure has two Es?

Which measures have C? ☐ and ☐

Which measures start with G? ☐ and ☐ and ☐

Can you play the score on piano?

STUDY D.s

What notes are missing on our staff?
Write in the missing notes.

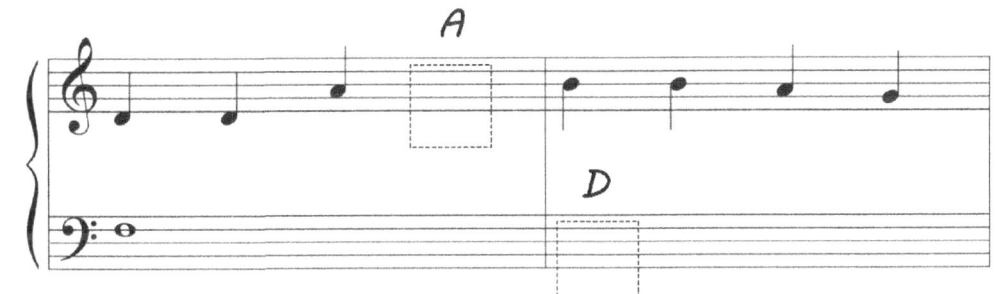

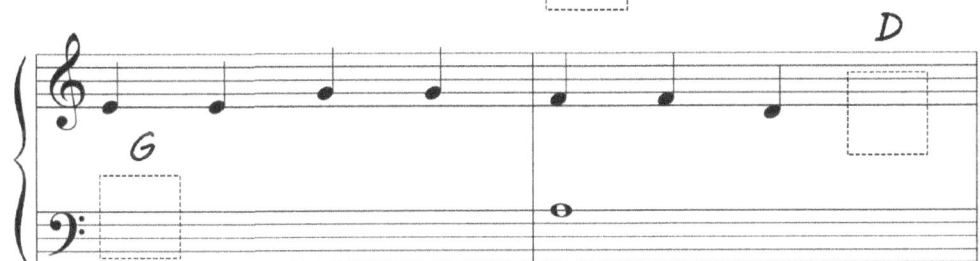

Great job!

Now play all the staves on the piano

CANON IN D MAJOR
by Johann Pachelbel

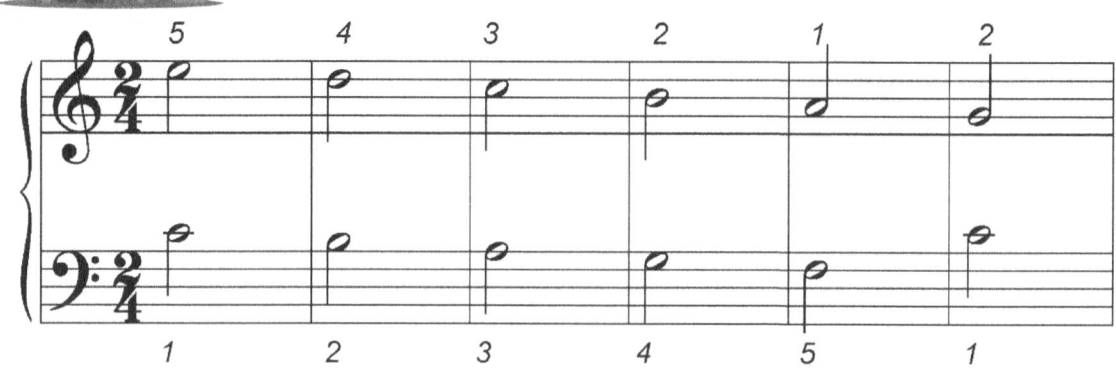

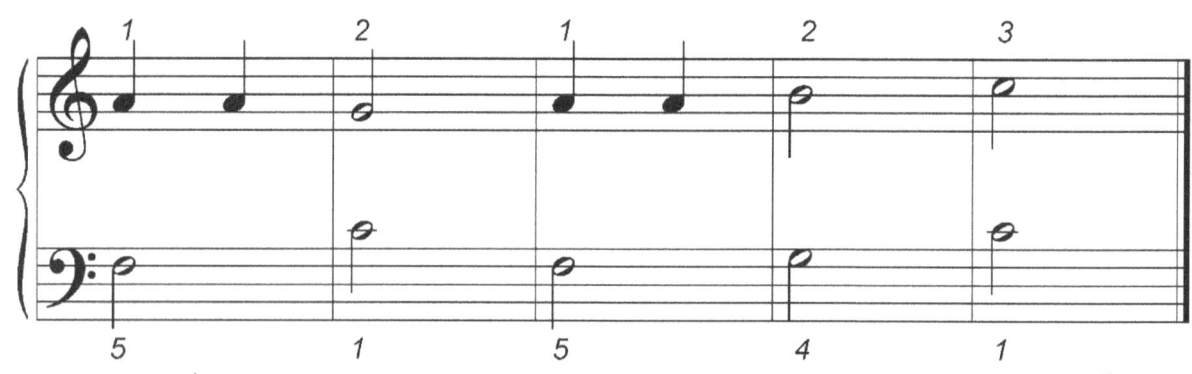

POP GOES THE WEASEL

Half a pound of tup-pen-ny rice,

half a pound of trea - cle.

Mix them up and make it nice

Pop! goes the wea - sel.

GO TELL AUNT NANCY

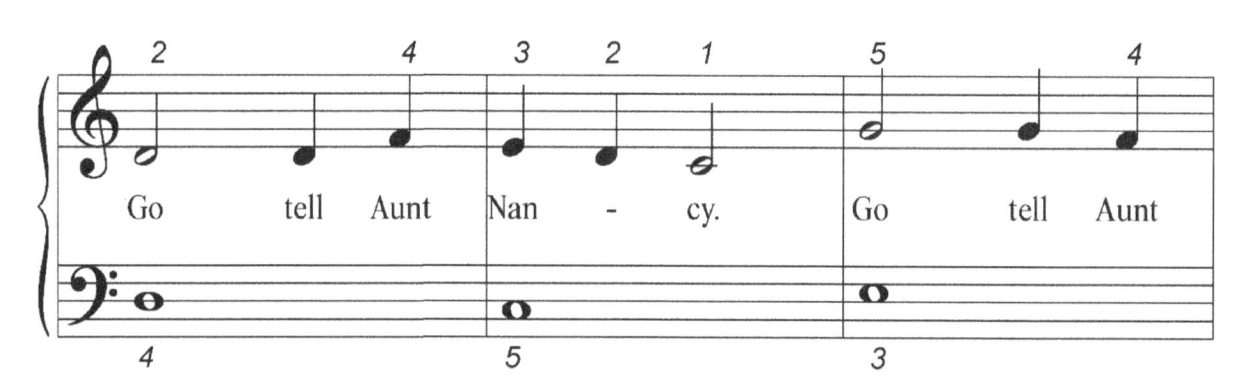

Go tell Aunt Nan - cy, Go tell Aunt Nan - cy. Go tell Aunt Nan - cy, the old gray goose is dead.

91

WHEN THE SAINTS GO MARCHING IN

Oh when the saints go march-ing in
Oh when the saints go march-ing in
how I long to be in that num-ber,
when the saints go march-ing in.

SPRING
by Antonio Vivaldi

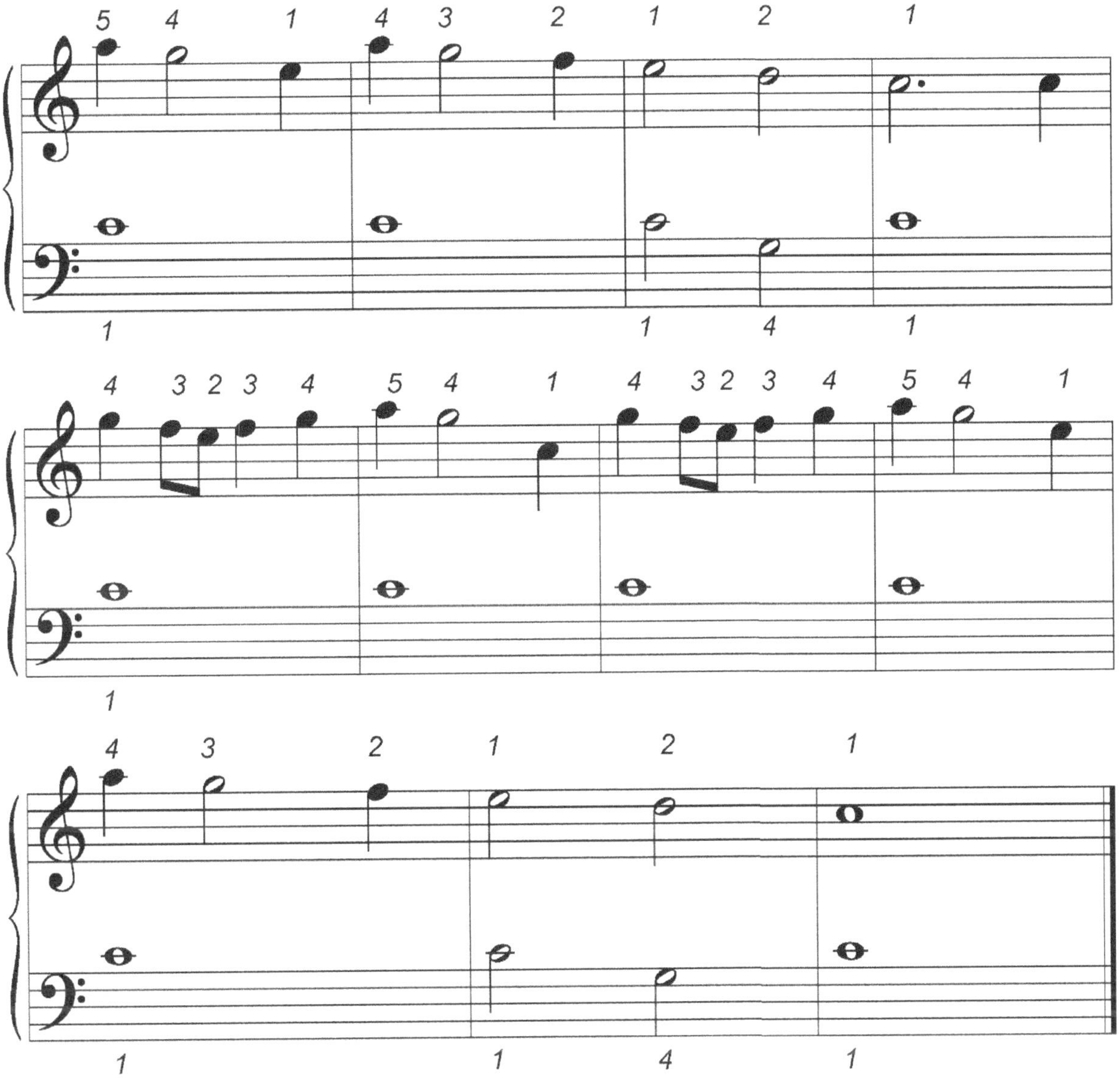

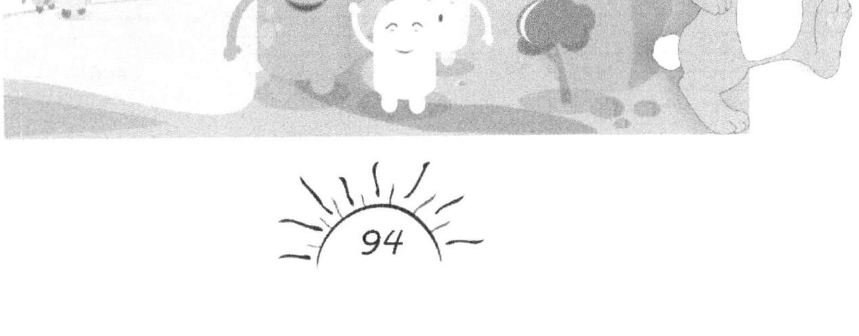

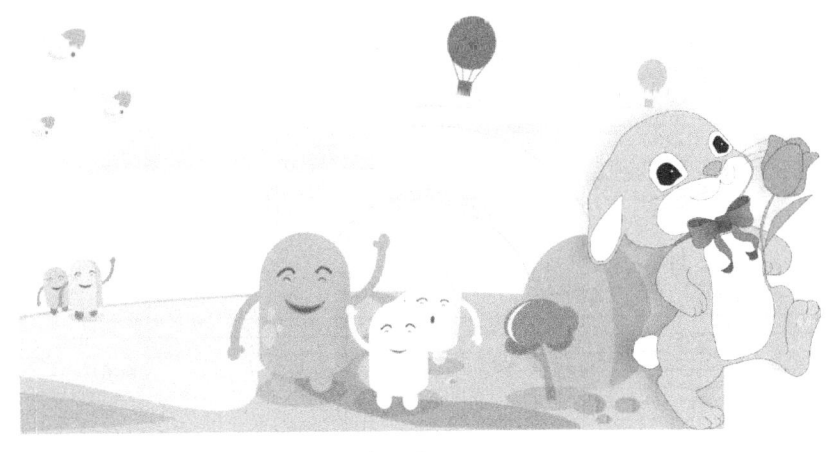

JOY TO THE WORLD

Joy to the world, the Lord is come! Let earth re-ceive her King; Let e-very heart, pre-pare Him room, and heaven and na-ture

sing, and_ heaven and na - ture sing, and_
hea - ven and - hea - ven and nat - ure sing!

SKIP TO MY LOU

Flies in the but-ter-milk, Shoo, fly, shoo,

Flies in the but-ter-milk, Shoo, fly, shoo,

Flies in the but-ter-milk, Shoo, fly, shoo,

Skip to my Lou my dar - ling.

ARE YOU SLEEPING?

Are you sleep-ing, Are you sleep-ing,

Bro-ther John, Bro-ther John,

morn-ing bells are ring-ing, morn-ing bells are ring-ing,

Ding, Dong, Ding! Ding, Dong, Ding!

98

HAPPY BIRTHDAY

Hap - py birth - day to you, Hap - py birth - day to you, Hap - py birth - day dear ...., ..., Hap - py birth - day to you.

THIS OLD MAN

LONDON BRIDGE

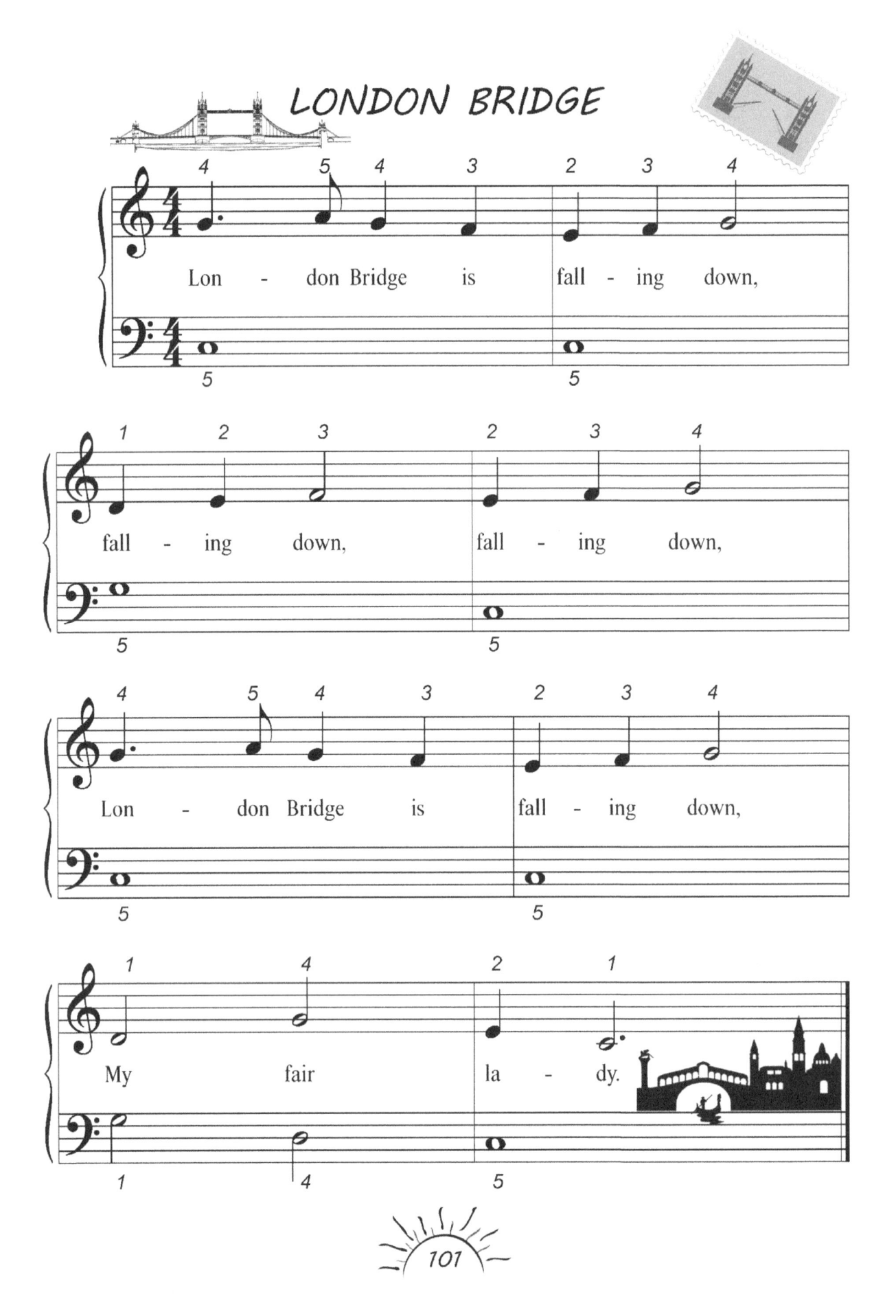

Lon - don Bridge is fall - ing down,

fall - ing down, fall - ing down,

Lon - don Bridge is fall - ing down,

My fair la - dy.

SHAVE AND A HAIRCUT

THREE CHINESE WITH A DOUBLE BASS

SILENT NIGHT

Si - lent night, ho - ly night,

all is calm, all is bright

round yon Vir - gin Mo - ther and Child,

ho - ly in - fant so ten - der and mild,

sleep   in hea-ven-ly peace

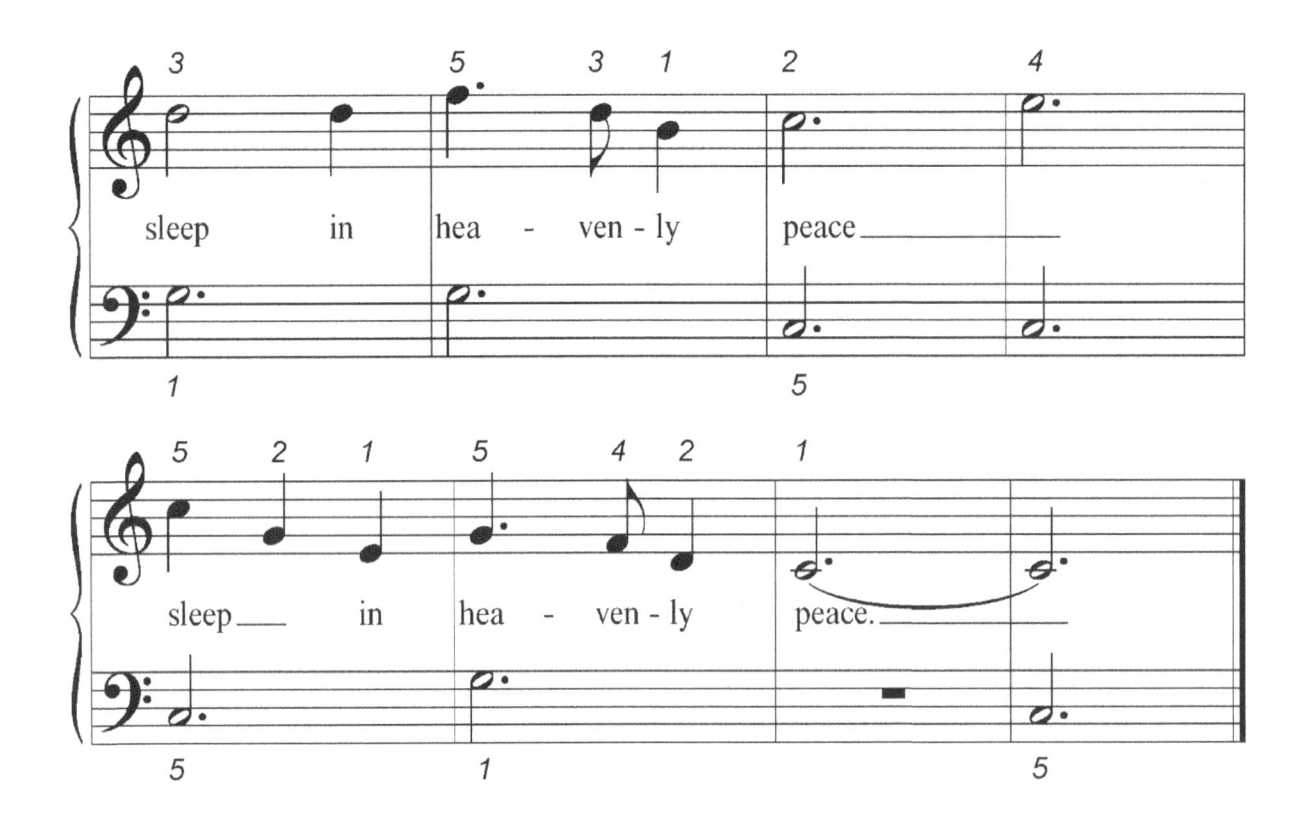

sleep   in hea-ven-ly peace.